THE
SWEATY
STARTUP

THE SWEATY STARTUP

How to Get Rich Doing Simple Things

NICK HUBER

Cornerstone Press

CORNERSTONE PRESS

UK | USA | Canada | Ireland | Australia
India | New Zealand | South Africa

Cornerstone Press is part of the Penguin Random House group of companies whose addresses can be found at global.penguinrandomhouse.com

Penguin Random House UK,
One Embassy Gardens, 8 Viaduct Gardens, London SW11 7BW

penguin.co.uk
global.penguinrandomhouse.com

First published 2025
001

Copyright © Nick Huber, 2025

The moral right of the author has been asserted

Penguin Random House values and supports copyright. Copyright fuels creativity, encourages diverse voices, promotes freedom of expression and supports a vibrant culture. Thank you for purchasing an authorised edition of this book and for respecting intellectual property laws by not reproducing, scanning or distributing any part of it by any means without permission. You are supporting authors and enabling Penguin Random House to continue to publish books for everyone. No part of this book may be used or reproduced in any manner for the purpose of training artificial intelligence technologies or systems. In accordance with Article 4(3) of the DSM Directive 2019/790, Penguin Random House expressly reserves this work from the text and data mining exception.

Designed by Yvonne Chan

Printed and bound in Great Britain by Clays Ltd, Elcograf S.p.A.

The authorised representative in the EEA is Penguin Random House Ireland,
Morrison Chambers, 32 Nassau Street, Dublin D02 YH68

A CIP catalogue record for this book is available from the British Library

ISBN: 978–1–529–93602–5 (hardback)
ISBN: 978–1–529–93603–2 (trade paperback)

Penguin Random House is committed to a sustainable future
for our business, our readers and our planet. This book is made
from Forest Stewardship Council® certified paper.

To everyone out there doing boring things to build a better life for their children and their children's children

Contents

Start Here   *ix*

Introduction   *xiii*

Part I: Opportunity

Chapter 1: Leverage   3

Chapter 2: Business Is a Race   23

Chapter 3: Not All Businesses Are Created Equal   38

Chapter 4: Idea Generation 101   52

Part II: The Skills

Chapter 5: Become an Expert Operator   73

Chapter 6: Sales Is the Foundation of Every Business   85

Chapter 7: Life Is Short   112

Chapter 8: Get Your Shit Together   127

Part III: People

Chapter 9: The Attributes of Winners   145

Chapter 10: How to Find High-Performing People   159

Chapter 11: Hiring—The Key to Ultimate Leverage   171

Chapter 12: Management and Delegation   189

Chapter 13: What Is This All About?   201

Conclusion   213

Acknowledgments   *217*

Start Here

Everybody thinks they need a revolutionary idea or a get-rich-quick scheme to find success. Something that has never been tried before. Something that will put a dent in the universe if it works and turn the founder into a billionaire and a walking legend. TechCrunch. Product Hunt. *Shark Tank*. Forbes 30 Under 30. All about *new* ideas. *Changing* the world. *Constant* innovation.

Business titans like Elon Musk and Mark Zuckerberg dominate social media, podcasts, and major publications preaching innovation and living on the cutting edge of technology. To hear them tell it, being an entrepreneur is all about 0 to 1. Blue ocean. Raising money. Infinite growth. Scalability and exits. Initial public offerings. Up and to the right . . . and on and on and on. You know what?

It's all garbage.

There's a radically different way of thinking about success, wealth, and entrepreneurship that has worked for millions of enterprising individuals since the beginning of time, and I will explain it to you in this book.

The most widely publicized path to wealth is what I just described, *but the most common path to wealth through entrepreneurship is actually by chasing a small, boring opportunity.*

Most of the wealthy people in your town who are eating at nice restaurants and have memberships at fancy country clubs didn't disrupt industries or raise venture capital. They started small, boring businesses.

I've met thousands of successful entrepreneurs. People flying around on private jets. People with vacation homes in the most expensive zip codes in America. People who play golf every day while earning more money than ever. People who spend time with friends and family and go on epic adventures with people they love.

What do they all have in common? *None of them had a new idea.*

These people are not famous. They weren't trying to change the world. They didn't raise venture capital. They didn't move to Silicon Valley to create viral apps. They aren't on the cutting edge of technology, and a few of them still have fax machines sitting in their offices. They do not spend time giving interviews to major publications, and nobody writes articles about them.

They go about their lives, running their businesses just a little bit better than their competitors.

Most of them started really small and traded their time for money doing actual work. A lawn care business is a sweaty startup. So are home service businesses, construction businesses, and trades. But mobile hairstyling can be a sweaty startup. Interior design, SEO, bookkeeping, video editing, or property appraisal companies are all sweaty startups, too.

What matters most isn't the type of business. It's that these entrepreneurs didn't reinvent the wheel—they stuck with proven business models that work.

Here's the kicker:

They kept going for five, ten, or twenty years. They built great businesses over time. They kept things simple. When they had more work than time to do it, they hired other people to help them for a few bucks less than they were charging. They managed risk and grew slowly. They built their skills and got better and better at making decisions related to business. They learned to lead other people. They became good at sales and persuading people to go along with them or buy from them.

One of them bought a car dealership and then bought ten more over the next fifteen years. Another took over a body shop from his father and turned it into a highly profitable chain of body shops. A third bought a struggling FedEx delivery route and transformed it into an empire. Yet another started an HVAC company twenty years ago and does more than $20 million in annual revenue today.

A friend of mine buys industrial buildings that were built by somebody else. He manages them a bit better and maximizes their profitability. That's it. That's the whole story. He's worth $250 million and he is thirty-six years old.

The stories you are about to read in this book are real. They are stories of actual people doing boring things for years. People doing hard things, making sacrifices, building skills, having fun, and getting rich slowly.

Most of these individuals have never spent a night in their offices on a cot. Less than half of them average more than forty hours a week after the first few years. None of them started the first or only company in their industry or even their town. All of them have competitors who are bigger and better than they are.

Most of them are just average people doing common things uncommonly well.

Entrepreneurship media has been lying to you, and this book is an official callout.

You do not need a revolutionary idea to become an entrepreneur.

I would go as far as to say with complete confidence that this mindset is sabotaging today's entrepreneurs and setting our next generation of business leaders up for failure.

Raising money and getting after a new idea are terrible ways to maximize your odds of success. Ninety-nine out of a hundred "new idea" startups fail. Most founders get discouraged by the entire process, think it is impossible to win as a business owner, and end up getting jobs.

I've watched it happen over and over again . . .

Above-average people with above-average skills try to start an incredibly hard business that nobody has been successful with before. They realize too late that no one has made *that idea* work yet because it's incredibly hard. They fail. They think they don't have what it takes, so they give up and go get jobs. It is *sad*. Motivated, talented people starting hard businesses, failing, and giving up on entrepreneurship forever.

Want to hear the most surprising thing about the wealthy people I know?

Most of the highly successful entrepreneurs and business owners I know today are totally normal people. They aren't brilliant. They don't have exceptional IQs. They did not score a 1530 on their SAT or go to a top-ten university. Many didn't even get a high school diploma.

Hell, some of them are even *below* average. Maybe even dumb.

What did they do well?

They were consistent. They delayed gratification. They put their egos aside and did things they didn't necessarily find interesting, fun, or exciting. They did something boring. They hired people and delegated. They were salespeople who sold themselves and their ideas to customers, partners, vendors, and employees. They picked a proven business model with weak competition and a lot of profit to go around.

They launched a sweaty startup.

Introduction

Entrepreneurship is undoubtedly the best way—and arguably the only way—to get seriously wealthy. If you want to get rich, trading your time for money won't work. You can't "save" your way to having enough to do whatever you want whenever you want.

If you had talked to me ten years ago, I would have told everyone to start a business.

You should do it! It is the only way to be happy. Working for somebody else is terrible!

Entrepreneurship culture has created an entire generation of people who dream about starting their own businesses. They don't want a job. They will not be happy working for somebody else.

But entrepreneurship isn't for everyone.

I have a stern warning for everybody reading this book:

Most people simply don't have what it takes to build their own businesses.

One of my greatest fears with my social media, this book, podcasts, and the rest of the work I do to spread the word about entrepreneurship is that I talk too many people into going down this road and starting companies they can't handle. Then they end up forty years old, divorced, and unhealthy with a failed business, no freedom, no wealth, and no hope. *Thanks a lot, Nick.*

The truth is that business ownership is brutal and stressful and requires a unique skill set that most people simply do not have and can't cultivate. The average person is unhealthy and broke and has poor relationships in every area of life. They are terrible decision makers. They are overweight. They can't handle a $500 surprise expense without borrowing money.

The average person can't manage their own life, let alone an organization with employees who depend on them, customers who buy from them, and the logistics, emotions, and problems that come with all of this.

When was the last time you read that in a book about entrepreneurship?

For most people, the best quality of life can be achieved by going to work for a good boss at a good company and earning good money with as little stress as possible. Most people don't thrive in chaotic environments. Most people hate sales. Most people are risk averse when it comes to finance. Most people can't handle life's uncertainty, let alone an organization with more than fifty individuals where every problem ends up on their desk.

If you are determined and you believe you might have what it takes, read on. This book is for you.

• • •

It was spring 2011. I was a junior at Cornell University taking an entrepreneurship course. I had twenty-four classmates, each with his or her own grand new idea. Big plans that required pitch decks and millions of dollars to fund untested dreams.

There I was. Student 25 with a boring, old-fashioned idea. One I put together based on businesses I interacted with or observed in my day-to-day life. I had merely half a page of notes at best. When my professor and classmates asked me what my differentiator was, I didn't have an answer.

I told them, "Students here on our campus can't stay in the dorms all summer. We're going to pick up their stuff and store it when they leave in May, and we'll return it to them when they get back in August. I'll answer the phone, do things a little better than the competition, and I think I can make some decent money."

They shook their heads.

"That isn't scalable," they told me. "It'll never be big. There are already a lot of companies doing it."

But if I didn't have "a vision," I did have *vision*. I saw a company in my college town doing pickup and delivery storage and making a lot of money doing it. I guessed more than $600,000 in revenue per year at 30 percent margins. They probably made almost $200,000 per year in profit just in Ithaca, New York.

And here's the thing:

They weren't very efficient at doing the actual work. They used clipboards. They didn't accept same-day appointments. Their employees sat around a lot. They didn't do much marketing. Their website was terrible. *Yet they made great money.*

My professor was right. The model wasn't scalable. It could never be "big" like Uber or Airbnb or Apple or Google. And there were more than twenty companies already doing this same work across the country.

But $200,000 per year was nearly three times the amount of money I stood to make by getting a normal job after college like all of my friends were doing.

> **Cold hard truth:**
> Entrepreneurship isn't about trying to change the world with the next scalable idea. It is about starting small, looking for a way to make good money doing something simple, and copying proven strategies that work.

My first company, Storage Squad, was a small idea in a crowded market that was nothing more than an opportunity to make a few dollars.

I handed out flyers with my phone number. I got a few people to pay me money for storage. And I used that money to grow the business. My first acquisition was a $1,500 cargo van with 170,000 miles on it. Otherwise I used the things I already had in my life to make some profit. That's it.

Contrary to what my professors told me to do and my classmates aspired to do, my idea and plan to execute were simple and unsophisticated:

- I wasn't trying to educate a customer base.
- I wasn't following my passion.
- I didn't need funding or a network.
- I wasn't competing against leading computer scientists from Stanford.
- I wasn't trying to prove a concept or create product-market fit.

I wasn't emotionally attached to anything except adding value to my customers and trading that value for money as quickly as possible.

My customers were out there, and my competitors existed. I could see them on campus and study their business models. I could watch how they operated, find out what they charged, uncover how they delivered value. And fairly quickly I could decide if I could do a better job or not. I could decide if there was an opportunity.

I made decisions with my brain, not my heart. I was competing against folks with fax machines, clipboards, and paper ledgers. All I needed to do to succeed was move a little faster and smarter. And here's the best part:

Storage Squad was profitable from day one.

Not a single one of the twenty-four folks in my class succeeded with their complicated or fantastical business ideas. Instead, they all went and got jobs. Their new ideas never caught on. They all had dreams of millions of users and billion-dollar exits. Scalable models that could work anywhere from a computer. But 99.999 percent failed to make a single dollar.

Something you should know about me:

I'm not brilliant or special. I scored 23 on my ACT and 1290 on my SAT. I don't know how to code. I wasn't born into a family of entrepreneurs or doctors or lawyers.

None of my partners or employees are brilliant or special. And you don't have to be brilliant or special either. There's another way to do business, to find success, and to keep things simple. I'm living proof this method works. It can work for you, too.

In this book, I'll share almost everything I've learned since 2011. But the short version is this:

Storage Squad made enough money in the early years that my partner and I were able to build our first self-storage facility. In January 2021, we sold Storage Squad for $1.75 million. We had no debt and no silent partners. My business partner and I split the cash.

Today, I own 50 percent of a company that controls (with our investors) sixty-eight self-storage facilities. More than two million square feet and $150 million of market value. In April 2024, I bought another company for $52 million. It is growing fast. I'm thirty-five years old and live in Athens, Georgia, with my wife and three kids (seven, five, and three).

I'm also involved in several additional companies, most of which I founded, which create multiple seven figures of personal cash flow each year. They are all boring businesses. Recruiting companies. A real estate services business. A marketing agency. Web development. Insurance. At the time of this writing, my net worth is somewhere around $50 million.

Net worth is a subject most people are afraid to talk about—it's a moving target. Truly wealthy people have *no idea* what their net worth is. They have most of their money tied up in assets that can't easily be sold or traded. They aren't like stocks with a constant mark to market that tells you what they're worth.

I'm not afraid to talk about money or net worth, and in my opinion you shouldn't be afraid either. You can discuss things without sounding arrogant if you frame them in the right way and bring them up at the right time with the right people.

I do not technically have a job in any of my companies. I am not the bottleneck. Small problems do not come to me, and there are no day-to-day tasks that require my time.

I spend my days making key decisions on the big stuff. *What return hurdles do we need to hit in order for a property to be a "buy"? Should we go after this new market or that new expansion opportunity? Should we hire this person and how should we design their compensation to set them up for success?*

I jump in and work hard when opportunities present themselves. I have spent the last few months in the weeds at my recruiting company building out a team in South Africa and changing the way we recruit and position our services. Next month I might be deeply involved in my real estate company chasing a new initiative or an acquisition. Some months I hardly work at all and spend a lot of time traveling or playing golf.

I don't say all of this to brag.

I say it because we live in a world where people (rightly) take advice and weigh it according to the strength of the source. So I would be doing myself a disservice not to tell you where I'm at in this game before I try to tell you how to win it.

Should you trust me and heed my advice blindly?

Absolutely not.

You should put everything you read here through your own personal bullshit detector and decide for yourself if you believe it or if it applies to you. But know this:

Business is dynamic. There are a thousand ways to win. People win in different ways every day.

There are thousands of important decisions you'll be tasked with making over the next several years. You'll get some of them wrong. You'll get some of them right. Your journey will not be like my journey. Your opportunities will be different. Your skills will be different. Not all of this stuff will apply to you, and a lot of it probably would not work for you.

But the good news is that some of it will.

I've divided this book into three sections—opportunity, skills, and people. These are the three most important factors in building a successful career and achieving what I consider to be the ultimate form of success and wealth:

Freedom.

Freedom to do whatever you want to do, whenever you want to do it.

You may have very little freedom today. You may not have the money to eat at a nice restaurant in town let alone travel to any hotel you want. You may be stuck going in to work at a job you dislike in an office you don't want to be in taking orders from a person you do not respect.

My goal is to help you change that.

In the first section, we'll talk about how to recognize great opportunities that most entrepreneurs pass over for being too hard and too boring. I'll let you in on the secrets of what kinds of businesses *not* to start, and I'll show you how to evaluate everyday businesses through a new lens. Then you'll assess your unique skills and situation and figure out what opportunities are right for you. Finally, you'll choose something and get started.

In the second section, we'll discuss the skills and mindset you need to build a company. It is hard to start a business. It is hard to grow a business. At the beginning, you will make sacrifices, and you will be stressed. That's the deal. But I learned how to manage the fear and stress, and I'll show you how to do the same.

In the third section, we'll talk about people. No one succeeds alone. Finding great people, selling them on your vision, and building simple systems so that people can succeed and win with you is difficult.

Your people will be one of your greatest assets because being able to delegate tasks and decisions is the path to freedom. And once you have freedom, the sky's the limit. You can sit back and enjoy the fruits of your labor or you can continue to build, seizing new and better opportunities armed with the skills, network, and capital to grow.

Everything you'll read here is my opinion, which has been shaped through my own personal experience. I've tried a lot of stuff. Some of it worked. A lot of it didn't. I've made decisions, failed, succeeded, and then used that feedback to adjust. I've changed my mind on a lot of things, and I will continue to do so for the rest of my life. And I've done the work.

I suggest you do the same. Forming your own opinions is uncomfortable. It requires deep introspection and questioning who you really are. Most people can't handle it. They simply follow the pack and get excited about what everyone else is currently excited about.

They believe what other people tell them to believe because it's a way to surrender responsibility and avoid accountability for creating the circumstances of their own lives.

So use successful people as a starting point, but not an end point. *Because most successful people don't actually have all the answers*. Instead, they are figuring it out as they go and making the best decisions they can based on a unique set of factors surrounding them at that very moment. They're very good at taking in data in an unbiased, unemotional way and then using it with clear heads and open minds.

They have strong opinions that are loosely held. This allows for flexibility. And anyone who's amounted to anything knows flexibility and being able to adjust your perspective put you leaps and bounds ahead of most people. Business strategy and management principles don't have sharp edges. There are none that work in every single situation. There are none that apply to everyone every time.

This means you shouldn't blindly listen to anyone. Even me.

You shouldn't look up to anyone as if they speak the absolute truth when it comes to business and management. And if those people tell you they are 100 percent sure they are correct, run the other way. Business is full of surprises, and no one can ever be certain.

The most successful people I know have been humbled by entrepreneurship.

Business is hard. Making money is hard. Everyone on social media will act as if it grows on trees and running a business is glamorous and stress-free.

It isn't.

The pressure is intense. You have families and people who depend on you to pay their rent. You have entitled customers who will belittle you. Negotiations won't always go your way. You'll make mistakes that cost you money when it hurts the most. And *every time* the phone rings, there is a problem that everyone is looking at *you* to solve. Uncomfortable conversation after uncomfortable conversation. People demanding more and more of you and more and more for themselves.

You won't get a call when things go well. Your employees will not thank you when the paycheck hits their account. Your customers will not thank you when you do what you promised. Nobody will think about you at all because they are too busy worrying about their own problems and their own issues.

With success comes a hell of a lot of stress, challenge, and responsibility. As you grow as an entrepreneur, you have a duty to your employees to guide them down the correct path.

It's extremely difficult, but for many entrepreneurs there's nothing else they'd rather do.

Part I
Opportunity

Leverage

I have a good friend who "won" the game.

He was the valedictorian of his high school. He went to Columbia. He almost made a perfect score on the LSAT. He graduated from Harvard Law School at twenty-six and moved to Washington, D.C., to work at Williams & Connolly, one of the most prestigious litigation firms in the world. He was crushing his job and getting assigned bigger and bigger trials. He traveled a lot. Spent more than fifteen days per month in courtrooms and hotels. By thirty years old, he earned more than $1 million per year and was on a clear path to becoming partner.

He was laying it all on the line, and from the outside he was winning big.

He got married, and he and his wife decided to start a family. She got pregnant and was scheduled to deliver in October 2022.

But in August of that year he was assigned to a high-profile case in

New York City that would go from September to December. He knew that if he took the case, he would be in a New York hotel or a courtroom when his wife went into labor. And that meant he would miss the birth of his first child.

He went into his boss's office and pleaded his case.

The partner told him to suck it up. He told him that attorneys at the firm had been making the same kinds of choices for fifty years. That in order to even be considered for partner in a few years, it was necessary to make sacrifices. The partner noted that my friend made seven figures a year and that thousands of attorneys would kill for the opportunity to work at this firm. Trade-offs like this were part of the price he had to pay. He had no other option but to do as he was told or get out.

My friend took a second.

The partner was the perfect embodiment of who he *did not* want to become. Fifty years old. Divorced. Overweight. Unhealthy. No relationship with his children and seventy-hour workweeks. Sure, he was rich. New Range Rover. Big house in the suburbs. Nicest country club membership. Giant beach house in the Outer Banks.

But no time to enjoy any of it.

The partner had zero control over his life. He had to miss family gatherings. He had to bend over backward for clients who were paying him millions. He had to answer to partners with more tenure than he had. He had sacrificed it all.

So my friend told the partner he was done, walked out of there that day, and changed careers altogether.

It was a sad, sad deal. My friend had sacrificed almost ten years of his life to be qualified to sit in the seat he was in. He had defied the odds. Scored in the top 1 percent on his exams. Gotten into the most exclusive schools in the country. He had worked seventy hours a week for four years. And busted his butt in law school before that. In theory, all his hard work had paid off. He was the best of the best.

He was *winning* the game.

> **Cold hard truth:**
> A lot of games that are glamorized by society aren't actually worth winning at all.

It took my friend far too long to figure that out.

Society will tell you to go to law school and lay it on the line. Your parents will encourage you to go to medical school. Or become a Big 4 accountant. But before you go into a specific career or a specific business, pick your head up and look around. Look at the corner office. What is life like for somebody who spends fifteen years winning the game you're about to play? Are they working sixty hours a week? Are they overweight, divorced, and stressed?

A lot of careers are like hot-dog-eating contests.

If you get really good at eating hot dogs, you get rewarded with more hot dogs.

Too many people are socially conditioned and pressured by those around them to play games where winning the game doesn't lead to a good life.

Status does not equal a good life.

In fact, it is often the opposite. Sometimes the more status that's associated with winning a game, the worse the quality of life is for the people who win.

Same goes for joining or launching a startup. Check the odds. A tiny number of people get very rich, sell their companies or take them public, and retire to the beach in their early thirties. But the vast majority flounder. They have moderate exits or jump from idea to idea without ever gaining traction. They sacrifice friends, family, and their health for a personal net worth that's never much more than they might have earned doing pretty much anything else.

If your goal is having enough money coming in every month so that you can do what you want to do when you want to do it, you have to play a game where winners are rewarded with money coming in every month while they do what they want to do when they want to do it.

And what winning means to me is choosing a career with a high return-on-time so that I can have freedom. A high return-on-time means that I work now and potentially get paid for a long time after the work slows down or stops. That leads to freedom. And if you have freedom, you can build a great life. Without freedom, it is virtually impossible.

If you are easily replaceable, do not own assets or shares in your company that make you money while you sleep, have no other options, and have people waiting in line to fill your spot, you have virtually zero leverage and your life will likely suck.

But if you are hard to replace, own assets or shares, have a lot of other options and nobody to fill in for you if you leave, you have a lot of leverage and you will be able to call the shots. What leads to a good life, flexibility, income, and the ability to seize opportunities worth going for is **leverage**.

Leverage is the key to life, so let's talk about getting some.

The Three Keys to Leverage

What is leverage?

Leverage is something that maximizes your advantage. Imagine a pulley system that makes lifting something heavy much easier. Or how a long lever and a fulcrum on which to place it allows you to move a large object with ease.

Life and business have examples of leverage, too.

A person can work alone for one hour and get only one hour worth of work done. But if they have forty employees, they can get forty hours of work done in one hour.

Most people have a small amount of leverage. They work two thousand hours a year in exchange for, say, $30,000. They trade one hour of their time for $15.

Other people with a large amount of leverage can work a thousand hours a year in exchange for $300,000. They trade one hour of their time for $300.

Some people have extreme leverage. They have several sources of income, and many of them are passive—meaning they do not need to do work or spend time in exchange for money. They have stocks that pay dividends, or they own real estate that somebody else manages while they collect the rent. No one decision from their boss or business partner can influence their quality of life. Nobody has power over them. They are insulated from risk because they are diversified.

Look around you. Who are the people *you know* with leverage and thus true freedom and wealth?

I'm not talking about the person who makes seven figures but is chained to a desk at a corporate job and lives for the weekend. I'm not talking about internet billionaires. And I'm not talking about the wealthy people you read about on the internet or in books.

Who are the wealthiest people *in your town*? Who are the people playing golf on Mondays or going on fishing trips on Wednesdays? Sure, money is important . . . up to a point. But I don't define wealth solely in terms of money. When I say "wealthy," I'm referring to the people *who do what they want to do when they want to do it*. These are the real entrepreneurs. These are the wealthy among us who have real leverage.

I have a friend who spent twenty years building a profitable business. He gets government contracts to run fiber internet and underground utilities. He also works with internet and utility companies to run the line alongside the roads. His first year in business he made about $100,000 in profit, or about $50 per hour for his time. He got his start trading time for money just as I did.

The company grew. By year five, he was making $750,000 personally, or about $375 for every hour he gave his business. By year fifteen, he was making more than $5 million in profit each year. Still working full time, forty hours a week. He had grown to more than 150 employees, and by then he was earning $2,500 for every hour he gave his business.

At year seventeen, three years ago, he hired a CEO to run the whole thing. His time is no longer required to run the business he founded, but he still owns almost all of it. And he makes more than $10 million each year. Now he travels, plays golf, and generally does whatever he wants.

His time leverage is nearly infinite. He gives his business virtually zero time but earns millions of dollars a year.

That is how leverage works.

I got talking to a gentleman recently at a cocktail party. He opened up and told me his story. He bought three rental properties with about

$60,000 of his own money in 2017. He still had a full-time job, but he did this on the side. Then he hired a property management company to run them so he wouldn't have to spend much time on the properties.

Now he makes $5,000 per month on those assets without ever having risked it all on a new idea in an uncertain marketplace. He chose a boring investment, and the income from those properties has given him a nearly infinite return on time and added a ton of freedom to his life. He still works his full-time job, which he enjoys, but he is one of many people who have started to gain leverage and stopped trading their time for every dollar they earn.

My lawyer friend was working seventy hours a week. Sure, he earned $1 million a year, but he had no control of his time. He couldn't work remotely. He had to get permission six months in advance for any vacation, and it could be canceled at a moment's notice for a trial. Hell, he was expected to miss the birth of his first kid.

If he stopped working, he stopped getting paid. If his boss said jump, he said how high.

He didn't have any leverage. His boss did. His clients did.

But many of the entrepreneurs I know work fewer than forty hours per week. They usually don't need to work more than ten, mostly between rounds of golf or for thirty minutes in the morning when they're traveling with family and friends. Some earn millions per year. They don't do manual labor. They could decide they want to go on a trip tomorrow, hop on the jet, and just go.

So what do my entrepreneur friends know that my lawyer friend had to learn the hard way? There's only one answer to that question: Leverage.

Leverage is what allows them to work so little and become wealthy while others are working so hard just to get by.

So how do we get leverage in all areas of life and business so that things get easier and we can begin operating at a high level? It depends on these three things.

1. Network

It isn't just about who you know, it's about who knows you.

To make money, you need other people to work for you, make decisions for you, help you, and partner with you. You need vendors. You need people to buy from you. You need investors and experts who can advise you. You need people you can reach out to who can add value to your life while you add value to theirs.

Your network is critical. Eventually, if you know people who know how to run companies, you can pay them to run your companies. If you know people with money, you can convince them to invest with you when you want to buy a property or an asset. If you know people who can work for your companies, they can recruit others to join them. If you know people who are connected, you will be somebody they think of when they spot an opportunity.

Very few people succeed in business alone.

2. Skills

How good are you at making things happen?

Building companies or accumulating assets that send you money every month takes skills. It requires a lot of hard decisions. It requires a certain mindset. It requires knowing how to do a lot of things.

Sales. Leading other people. Hiring. Management. Delegation. Decision making. Without experience or practice, you don't have any of these skills. People aren't born with the ability to lead other people. The same goes for hiring, delegating, decision making. They suck at all of it. But if you can build skills that nobody else has, then you are hard to replace and people need your expertise.

So how do you gain the skills? You get out and practice. All the important skills we will discuss in this book are muscles. If you wanted to build muscle like Arnold Schwarzenegger, what would you do? Read about muscles, spend your time making workout plans, get all the necessary supplements and powders, watch videos of Arnold, and *think* about building muscles? No. You'd go to the gym and lift weights. It's the same for business.

Reading this book won't help you unless you get out and put some of this stuff into action. Skills are acquired in the gym by lifting the weights.

3. Capital

Let me tell you a secret:

It is ten times easier to build a great business when you aren't strapped for cash in your personal life. If you can run your company without worrying about paying your bills or putting food on the table, it is a massive advantage. You can make payroll without stress. You can invest in equipment and marketing. You can invest in growth without increasing your stress.

How much cash do you have in the bank? How much cash do you have coming in every month?

Cash flow lets you hire people, make investments, and, most important, take risks. You will be at a disadvantage as an entrepreneur unless you have personal cash flow coming in the door to support your life. At the beginning, you may have little to no cash flow, but from the moment you are cash flow positive, your life begins to get easier and less stressful.

Entrepreneurs who are wealthy from previous endeavors are able to move faster, invest in growth, and hire ahead of revenue. They can grow companies much faster than a broke bootstrapper who needs to live on their company in the early days and can't afford a mistake.

• • •

Business is a chicken-and-egg problem in all three of these areas. It is a massive advantage to do business when you have the network, skills, and capital to grow quickly, but you can't get the network, skills, and capital until you've practiced and built a company.

The most successful entrepreneurs play business on easy mode and achieve leverage because they have slowly and steadily acquired the network, skills, and capital to do so. They are good at doing what needs to be done to make money. They started with a disadvantage and slowly built their advantage.

It takes time and it takes effort. You can't build leverage overnight and grow a network, skill set, and income streams out of thin air. Think of leverage like a ladder. There are rungs on the ladder that lead to higher and higher levels of leverage and thus success. You can't skip steps. It is a process.

The No-Asshole Rule

When you have very little leverage, you have to do what you have to do. Bend over backward for customers. Deal with disrespectful partners. Take investments from folks who don't have the same vision as you do and adjust the terms to their liking. But as you build enough experience and wealth, this slowly shifts.

How do you know you've made it?

You get to stop doing business with assholes. You have the leverage to remove yourself from any situation of your choice.

No asshole clients. No asshole partners. No asshole investors. You can start firing bad customers. Breaking up with bad partners. And buying out bad investors. Because leverage isn't just about creating and seizing opportunity. It also allows you to build your tribe and spend time with people who want to make you better and win with you.

When you start, you have no leverage and no advantage because the people around you have everything you need and you are a commodity. But when you get some skill and experience, the scales begin to tip in your favor.

It starts slowly. Every once in a while you realize that not just anyone can do what you can do. So you negotiate more for yourself. And then, over time, you aren't a commodity anymore, and what's even stranger is that sometimes the other person becomes the commodity.

It's beautiful. From having no power at all at the beginning, now you get to set the terms, and the other person doesn't get to act like an asshole. If they do, you're gone. Clients need you more than you need them. Partners need you more than you need them. And when you get really good, something amazing happens.

Business gets easier. You start to make even more money. You get to work on even more exciting things. And then you get even more leverage. And even more money.

And the snowball continues to roll down the hill.

• • •

My own journey toward leverage was a slow, tedious grind that took place over more than ten years.

During the first years of both Storage Squad and my self-storage business, I spent many hours on the phone with asshole customers who yelled at me. No matter how worn out, frustrated, and beaten down I felt at the end of one of those days, it didn't matter. I couldn't afford to hang up on them or fire them because I desperately needed the money they had. And they knew it.

The same thing with investors. In the early days of real estate, I took money from anybody and everybody. I offered the terms they requested. When they told me to jump, I asked how high. They knew they had leverage and could treat me that way. I needed their money more than they needed me.

But today I own several companies that produce more than $500,000 of monthly income for me personally, and I have a unique skill set. People need me more than I need them. And where I used to have no leverage, in more and more situations I find that I have it all.

For example, I had an investor a few years ago who was being a complete pain in the ass. Not disrespectful, just a pain. Asking a ton of repetitive questions. Constantly emailing us to find out what we were doing to improve operations at a specific storage facility. Requesting calls with me personally.

We regularly spent thirty minutes on the phone talking through the intricate details of every deal he was involved in, but no matter how much attention we gave him, it wasn't enough. I could tell from experience that he was stressed and was likely in a bad situation financially.

At the time we had more than three hundred active investors, and this one guy was about 50 percent of our email inbound over the course of a few months.

So I bought him out. I offered to buy his shares and return the $300,000 he had invested. He accepted, I cut him the check, and we deleted him from our database. He wasn't an asshole, but the whole interaction was more trouble than it was worth.

Luckily, I had the leverage (personal cash flow) to remove him from our company.

Several years ago, a guy approached me to buy one of my self-storage facilities. He offered a price that I believed was higher than its actual value, so I agreed to sell him the property.

About a week into discussions he began acting totally unprofessional. Calling me at random hours and yelling at me for not providing certain documents or being available at specific times to show him a building. Now, I'm not one to get my feelings hurt, but he was borderline emotionally abusing me on the phone. I could tell this was his plan all along and he does this in many areas of life and business.

He was an asshole.

So what did I do? I terminated the contract. *Sorry, bud. I don't need your money bad enough to justify this headache. See ya!* We still own the property today, and it is performing well, making me money each and every month.

Finally, we had a customer at my web development firm, WebRun, throw a fit halfway through a project. He told us our work was horrible. This part of the website was bad. We needed to improve this, that, and the other thing. He said our work was totally unacceptable.

Before you assume the worst, let me tell you, I can handle feedback. My employees can handle feedback. We welcome collaboration with customers, want to do the best work in the industry, and have a ton of happy customers at WebRun. I couldn't help but think that something was off.

My partner and operator at WebRun filled me in on the details. I looked at the work. It was good. The customer was in the wrong and was the only unhappy customer the company had had to date. We had done more than forty projects from start to finish.

Ten years before, I would have done whatever it took to satisfy this client. But some people won't ever be satisfied. They enjoy having power and using it. This client didn't realize that we have a lot more leverage than we let on, so we decided to fire him and send his money back. We didn't need him enough to put up with his abuse. *See ya!*

Operating from a position of leverage is a cheat code to a happy life. When you have leverage, you have options. You have your own capital. You can pay your own bills. You can do what you need to do not just for your business but for your peace of mind.

If you don't need to take money from assholes, you can rid your life of them completely. And when you never have to do what another grown human tells you to do if you don't want, that's when life gets fun.

Return on Time

There are two questions you should be asking about any opportunity you are considering going after:

- What is the return, in dollars, for an hour of my time today, a year from now, and ten years from now?
- If I stop working, do I stop getting paid or will I keep getting paid?

That's it. The answers to those questions will tell you all you need to know about the choices you're making. Here is a simple example:

If I go to McDonald's and trade my time for $15 an hour flipping burgers, what is the return on that time? It is $15. A year from now it will be $16.25. Ten years from now it will be about $25 per hour if I become a manager.

What happens if I stop giving my time to McDonald's? I stop getting paid. No more of my time, no money.

Now let's keep going. *What if I were a franchisee and I owned a McDonald's that I staffed with local employees to run for that same $15 an hour? If I didn't go to work that day or week, would I still be making money?*

Of course I would. In fact, I'd be making a lot more than just $15 an hour. The average McDonald's franchisee makes about $300,000 per year per location. That number will likely be higher a year from now and a lot higher ten years from now.

Let's imagine another scenario. *If I start today to build a business, and I trade my time for money, what is the return on that time?*

It is the hourly wage you charge for your work, whether that's solar panel installation, boat cleaning, home appliance repair, photo booth rental, or any number of other boring businesses.

And if I spend five to ten years building a business, hire employees, and turn over operations to a great CEO, and then I stop, what is my return on time?

It could be millions of dollars a year for the rest of my life. I could end up with a business that runs without my energy and time and makes me money while I sleep.

If your goal is wealth and doing what you want to do when you want to do it, you need to consider if your current career path lends itself to getting paid even if you're not working at some point in the future. If your answer is no, then it's time to stop doing what you're doing and start building the leverage you need to change that.

The amount of money you earn is not correlated with how hard you work. It is correlated with how hard you are to replace and thus how much leverage you have.

If you are easy to replace, then you have low leverage and a capped earning potential. But if you are impossible to replace, you have high leverage and unlimited earning potential. So your goal should be to start a business (or businesses) and get to a point where people need you more than you need them. But it doesn't happen overnight.

I've had this conversation hundreds of times, so I know what you're thinking. *Nick, I don't have any leverage. How do I get some? What is my plan?*

Ask yourself, *Does this career or what I'm doing today have the potential to create passive income and thus leverage for me in the future?* If it does, keep going. If it doesn't, it's time to step back and reevaluate.

Here's why:

At some point in the future, if you have money coming in the door that you don't have to work for, that creates leverage. Though it might seem far-fetched now, if you have $50,000 a month coming in from three sources you control, and you spend $20,000 per month on your life, you have all the leverage you need. There won't be a single human being who can control your life enough to mess it all up if you don't do what they say.

Unfortunately, many of the high-status professions we've been guided toward aren't all they're cracked up to be. Med school equals zero leverage. A doctor, unless they invest saved capital into other things, has no ability to stop working and continue to get paid. It is very hard for them to separate their time from money and start working ten hours a week in their forties with enough income to do whatever they want.

Actually, 99 percent of professions have zero leverage. There are a few like wealth management, insurance, and sales that create passive income into the future long after the work is done—I love those careers. But for the most part, if you work a W-2 job, you will forever be trading your time for money.

So what is your first goal? How do you get started?

You start small. You get $2,000 per month coming in from something you own (either a side hustle or a small business or a piece of real estate). Then keep doing that thing to turn that $2,000 into $5,000 over the course of a few months or years. Then $10,000. Then $20,000, and suddenly you can tell your boss to go shove it next time he tells you to do something you don't want to do.

And then you have the leverage.

It's Time to Redefine Success

What does success look like to you? What is true wealth? What situation is a win for you to be able to live a happy life?

In this book I'll ask you to do a few simple exercises. This is the first one.

Get out a piece of paper or open your laptop and write down the answers to the following questions:

Where do you live? How much are you working? What do you do on Monday at 9:00 a.m.? What does your week look like? How are you spending your *time*?

Go ahead and make a list, make a spreadsheet, do this exercise for real. I'll wait.

Now, imagine your perfect week if money were no object and you didn't need to work to bring it in. Ask yourself the same questions. Write down the answers.

Build your ideal life.

Are you done? Okay, here's what I've been trying to say about wealth:

It's not just about money, it's about freedom. True wealth is being able to do what you want, when you want, without being chained to a desk or beholden to someone else's schedule.

When you look at what your week looks like, what do you see? Can you do what you want when you want to, or are you stuck doing things you don't want to do *every single day*?

Let's face it:

Ninety-nine percent of people spend their careers doing things they don't want to do to support a lifestyle they get to live in the evening, on weekends, ten vacation days a year, and on federal holidays—if they're lucky.

They get out of bed and go to work, and some other grown human tells them what to do, how to do it, and when they can go on vacation. Ultimately, it doesn't matter how many dollars you have in the bank if someone else has more control over your life and time than you do.

True wealth is a function of time and money.

Show me a person who makes $1 million a year but is chained to a desk for seventy hours a week to earn that money, and I'll show you somebody who is *not* wealthy. Now show me another person who makes $150,000 a year but works five hours a week, rides mountain bikes around Colorado all summer, and fishes in the Florida Keys all winter, and I'll show you somebody who is *very* wealthy.

Now part two of this exercise:

How much money do you need coming in every month after taxes to make your ideal lifestyle happen?

Write down all of the monthly expenses it would take to live your dream life. For example, $5,000 on a mortgage, $4,000 for food, vehicles, and health care. Keep going. Include your travel, fun, hobbies. Literally everything. Now add it all up. How much are you spending?

My answer to this question when I was twenty-five years old was that I needed $20,000 per month coming into my bank account after taxes, and my goal was to work five hours a week to get it. It took me five years, but I achieved this by age thirty. Money doesn't go as far today as it did in 2014, so that number is more like $30,000 per month in today's dollars.

My ideal lifestyle was pretty simple. With $360,000 coming in every year, I could live in a nice house with room for five kids in a great town. I could send them to a good school. I could drive reliable, safe vehicles. I could order what I wanted to from most restaurants, and I could do a little bit of travel. I could join a nice country club and play golf a few days per week. I could do whatever I wanted with my friends and loved ones.

I didn't need a private jet. I didn't need a ten-thousand-square-foot house. I didn't need a loaded Escalade or a brand-new truck. I didn't need lavish things, and I still don't. You probably don't need those things either.

What is your number?

I'm willing to bet that what you need to achieve true wealth, to achieve leverage, is a number far lower than what you imagine. Because freedom isn't ultimately about money. Freedom is about leverage and time. If you have leverage and time, you can go wherever you like. You can exercise and keep your body fit and strong. You can be a great spouse and parent. You can spend time with whoever you want and make epic memories with people who matter to you.

Right now it might all feel like a distant dream. You might be at the start or in the middle of building a company and have no idea what you're doing. You might not have any or many assets that can produce money when you're not working. This is why the number you've just settled on matters so much.

Pretend you're a poker player thinking about chip allocation during a tournament.

You're playing the odds with a finite number of resources to invest in different opportunities. Your chips are your time. And you have only so much of it. How will you invest that time? What hands will you play and what hands will you fold? What opportunities will you chase and what opportunities will you ignore?

The million-dollar question:

What can I do right now that maximizes my odds of making the money I need to live the life I want five years from now? How can I invest my hours in a day (that is, my chips in front of me in a poker game) in the opportunities (cards) that are most likely to lead to success?

When I asked myself that question, I knew one thing for sure:

It wasn't a W-2 job. And it wasn't a venture-backed startup. Most regular jobs would never have gotten me where I wanted to go because 95 percent of startups fail after their founders and employees invest most, if not all, of their chips. Five to ten years down the drain and no residual income. The venture-backed startup was the highest odds of making $1 billion. But I didn't have a goal of $1 billion. I didn't need the status. I just needed $30,000 coming in every month without being chained to a desk.

It was a singular focus.

What opportunities was I going to chase to maximize my odds of making $30,000 per month within five years?

That was my goal and that was my big question. It wasn't a job. It wasn't a tech startup.

What was it?

It was a sweaty startup. A boring business. I picked up boxes and dropped them off and charged people money for it. I got out and I got after it.

Chapter 2

Business Is a Race

It was the fall of 2011. My business partner Dan Hagberg and I had just started Storage Squad a few months earlier. We were fifty-fifty partners, and we were starting our senior year of college.

As the months ticked by, we watched all of our friends at Cornell get big money jobs in New York City and Chicago. Investment banking. Hedge funds. Fortune 500s. Big 4 consulting. Their offers started at $80,000 and went up to $120,000 per year.

We knew our Ivy League degrees were worth something and there was a serious opportunity cost for every week we spent moving boxes when we could be kicking off successful careers at big companies.

The business was about eight months old, but I still wasn't sure if I could hack it as an entrepreneur. People told me I was crazy. Nobody else was doing this. And frankly, there is something uncomfortable about going in a totally different direction from literally everyone else in your life. No matter how confident you are, that sense of anxiety and fear creeps in, and I'll admit that it got to me. So I decided to keep my options open and run a job hunt at the same time I was building my company.

Halfway through my senior year, I received an offer from Coca-Cola in Irvine, California, for $80,000 per year. That was a lot of money right out of school in 2012. At the time, my partner and I had one cargo van and $5,000 in total revenue.

I called my father and told him I was considering going all in on Storage Squad.

He was surprised and apprehensive. He mentioned a few of my friends with big-time job offers. He reminded me my Ivy League degree was valuable and that I was the first kid from Perry County, Indiana, to ever graduate from *any* Ivy League school. He was nervous.

"You're using your Ivy League degree to drive a moving truck," he said. "You know I support you, but you better make it count."

Dan was fielding similar offers, so right then and there we set a goal for ourselves. We needed to either fail spectacularly or make something happen. The worst-case scenario was a failed business after burning five years of valuable time. There is no slow rolling entrepreneurship when you could be earning $80,000 a year and starting a career in corporate America.

So we decided to get uncomfortable. We would focus on speed. We made a big plan and started racing.

Instead of just operating at Cornell, we would launch at three other major universities. We convinced three people in our network—Dan's cousin at Illinois, my best friend, who was in grad school at Indiana, and Dan's best friend, who was an undergrad at Iowa—to open and run branches of our business there. We made a wild guess on a profit-sharing plan with our friends who would do the work on the ground.

Then we took a few more of our student loan dollars and bought three more cargo vans.

Our singular goal was to get more than 250 customers that spring.

If we did that, we would prove—to ourselves and the world—that Storage Squad was a viable business and that sticking with it was a rational choice.

So we wrote "250" really big on the whiteboard in Dan's room. And we agreed that if we couldn't get 250 customers, we would shut down the business and go get jobs. Two hundred customers wasn't good enough. Two hundred forty-nine wouldn't even be sufficient. It was 250 or bust. That was our high-water mark. It was our "proof of concept."

The discomfort was almost unbearable. We had no idea what we were doing. How would we compensate our employees? Where would we store the stuff? Where would we get the money to lease warehouses and buy boxes?

Oh, and did I mention all of this would be happening during finals week our senior year? And that Dan and I were finishing our Division I track careers? We were both captains, and I had been a DI All-American the previous year.

Not only was I trying to finish the season strong, I was also training hard, hoping for an Olympic trial run and another Ivy League championship in the decathlon. Most important, I had met a girl a few months earlier who I wanted to marry. So I was busy selling her on spending her life with me.

But by the end of May, it was done, and I had a plan for what was going to happen next. I passed all of my finals and graduated with a 3.4 GPA from an Ivy League school. I won the decathlon at the conference championships with a school record, and I got eleventh at the USA championships. I told that girl I loved her at graduation, and she said it back. She's my wife today, and we have three kids. I missed the Olympic trials by one spot and hung up the spikes, but I was preoccupied enough with other exciting things that I couldn't have cared less. Storage Squad ended the season with 253 customers. Dan and I had a heart-to-heart, promised each other we wouldn't get jobs, and kept racing ahead full speed.

You may think that the urgency I'm describing is a young person's game. Something that's only possible when you're in your twenties and eager and have something to prove. But my entire entrepreneurial career has been a race ever since.

And your entrepreneurial career is a race, too.

You have a lot of mistakes to make. A lot of things to learn. Experience is invaluable and there is only one way to get it.

Time.

Time is your most valuable asset and your most valuable resource. You can't get it back. You can't rewind. You are getting older. You need to get your business off the ground quickly, so you can learn more, improve your skills faster, and become successful. That's because one of your primary goals (if not *the* goal!) is to figure out if your business is going to support your life in as little time as possible. If it can't, move on. If it can, keep investing.

Here's the bad news:

I moved uncomfortably fast and I still made less than $15 per hour for that entire first year—about $30,000 all in. And it was hard, stressful work. Way harder and way more stressful than the work my friends were doing making three to five times the money.

The second year wasn't much better, at about $25 per hour, or $50,000 of pretax profit. More stress. More discomfort. It was a crash course in what not to do. Business came at us fast. I made every mistake in the book.

But I learned, kept a positive attitude, and kept chugging away. The next year I finally outearned my friends by a little bit. The year after that by a bit more. Then a few years later we built the self-storage facility. And a few years after that I got rich when that facility became a lot more valuable and we sold our business.

I stayed in the game. I maintained confidence and brought the energy. I moved fast, raced, and ended up getting the snowball rolling down the hill. I was gaining speed and momentum.

The mistake people make is that they want to stay comfortable, so they move too slow. They keep it too small for too long so that the twenty-four months it took me to break into "above-average compensation" never comes or takes five years. In the end, they can't make it that long, so they give up and go get jobs.

Act Now and Ask Questions Later

It's simple.

If you aren't rich yet, your first (or your fifth or your tenth) business should be profitable in the first six months.

If it isn't profitable or it isn't a business model that has the potential to be profitable, go do something else. Your opportunity cost is too high, and time is your most valuable asset.

The most successful people don't sit around planning all day. They live with a sense of urgency. They don't aim, aim, aim, aim, aim, fire. They aim, fire, aim, fire, fire, fire, and ask questions later.

Perfect has been and always will be the enemy of progress.

I had a friend at Cornell who was very serious about entrepreneurship. He was always scheming, planning, researching, thinking about new ideas. He read countless books on entrepreneurship, took every class at Cornell on the subject, listened to thousands of podcast episodes, studied the biographies of every great entrepreneur who ever lived.

Every time I spoke to him, he wanted to talk about a new idea he was considering. He would spend two months studying a subject, talking to potential customers, and building marketing and business plans before giving up and moving on. This was the case literally all four years of college. He ended up graduating, going to get his MBA, and continuing his great research project trying to figure out what business to start.

Several times my friend got close to taking the leap. He built websites. Got T-shirts made. Won pitch competitions. He was a software guy and actually built a few apps. He created the MVPs and was well down the road with a few of the projects. He even got close to raising money and making it happen for real with some hiring and trying to find customers.

But each time he'd get cold feet. He'd find ten reasons or a hundred reasons why the business idea was flawed. He'd learn something important that made him change his mind and realize the company could never work. Then he'd be back to the drawing board. More analysis. More planning. Never pulling the trigger. Today my friend works in corporate America and still has that dream of someday founding a disruptive, scalable company.

I bet you know someone like my friend. You might even *be* someone like my friend. Analysis paralysis is very common in entrepreneurship. People sit back and read, study, analyze, calculate, think, worry, get excited, and then when it comes time to actually get started, they get cold feet.

The analysis paralysis you feel is largely based on a flawed way of thinking that says everything has to be perfect before you can get started. That the idea, timing, and business plan will make you either a winner or a loser. That is wrong.

> **Cold hard truth:**
> Execution is a thousand times more important than your idea. Hiring. Delegation. Selling. Logistics. Communication. The boring stuff.
> That's what the winners get right.

When you are just getting started, business is a race. Your competitors are already making moves. Every opportunity is a small window in time and the door closes quickly. If you hesitate, if you second-guess yourself, you've missed it. It's over. You just finished your business plan and finally got off the couch when the door slammed in your face.

So go *now* and chase the opportunity.

I had an insanely resourceful college kid ask me to get lunch a few years back in Athens, Georgia. She was an undergraduate at UGA, and she was interested in starting a recruiting firm in the construction industry because her father had a big construction company and she had some ins with other owners.

Over lunch I told her to get after it. Cold-call five owners to see if they would pay her to find them employees. Lunch ended and that was that. A year later, she reached out to share that she was doing $30,000 per month of revenue and had an assistant she'd just hired into her recruiting company. It was growing fast. She did most of the work herself. It wasn't a revolutionary idea. She just got her hands dirty and built a business.

Every phenomenally successful person I've met shares this trait of bias toward action. They know opportunity when they see it. They aren't afraid to move fast. They trust their gut. They start with low-risk decisions, improve at the art of making decisions, and then eventually make them quickly, which creates momentum, a key factor for success.

Small disclaimer:

Don't act recklessly. Your preparation time should be correlated with the amount of risk you are taking. If you're making a significant investment in time or capital to start or grow your business, stop to think before you jump. For example, if you're buying a $50,000 piece of equipment, do your homework. But if you're considering a low-risk endeavor like power washing a neighbor's sidewalk or helping a friend haul junk to the landfill, get off the couch and go!

The weight and risk of decisions increase with time. At the beginning, mistakes won't set you back as far as you think. I made countless poor decisions and boneheaded moves in 2012 during that first year in business. But I'm here. That's because real entrepreneurs try stuff out the same day they think of it. They go ask customers to pay them money. They get their hands dirty and get sweaty trading their time for money servicing early customers. They fail quickly and start again if they can't make it happen.

In my experience that's what works best and what I did myself. I jumped in when I saw an opportunity, and my partner and I were off and running on Storage Squad insanely quickly. After two weeks of hard work at the end of junior year, I had $5,000 cash sitting on my bed and was on a mission to grow a boring little service company.

Analysis paralysis is a horrible disease. Don't let it infect you.

Stop Worrying What Other People Think

I know a lot of below-average people who make phenomenal money simply because they aren't insecure. They are confident enough in themselves and their own abilities to move forward regardless of other people's opinions. They aren't afraid of failure. They don't spend time feeling sorry for themselves or second-guessing what other people might think of them if they do a certain thing.

There is a very simple, easy way to develop thick skin:

Practice.

Just kidding. It actually isn't easy. But it works. You have to take risks, put your neck out, and do uncomfortable things. You have to have people treat you poorly and get jealous. Then you have to shake it off and recover and get used to it. Because when you do different things, and especially when you win, people *will* get jealous. They'll feel bad about themselves. They'll work to tear you down and say negative things about you. It's just a fact of life.

So you have to practice letting it roll off your back. You have to move along to the next project, obstacle, uncomfortable situation, and insult. And with time, it will hurt less, you'll recover faster, and you can go about your business.

I know because I've had *a lot* of practice.

I was bullied hard in elementary and high schools. Kids were cruel to me and humiliated me in front of my peers, which is unfortunately very common.

But it didn't end there. Right around the time Dan and I were busting our butts to try to make Storage Squad work, I sat down one afternoon at the entryway of the locker room before track practice to change my shoes. Nobody knew I was there.

Some of the guys on the team were chatting it up. They were the fastest, got the girls, and had jobs lined up after college at prestigious companies. I quickly realized they weren't talking about just anything. They were full on making fun of *me* and my business.

"We're out here getting offers at Goldman in N.Y.C. while Huber is driving a fifteen-year-old van around town moving boxes. I give that business one year max. He'll end up working for a moving company for the rest of his life. What a dumbass."

I froze before silently backing out of the locker room and changing for practice in my car. It was hurtful and made me feel like total shit.

But then what?

I went about my business. I let the pain subside. I stayed the course. I got done with practice and went to dinner with my buddies.

I got over it and never said a thing to those guys.

If you're doing something unique, you *will* be a target. If you're creating your own version of success and taking risks, people notice. And they judge. Especially when you make mistakes and look foolish from time to time. But winners aren't afraid to do a few cringe things now and then. To step down a few rungs on the ladder and work hard at something that isn't high status or sexy. That is the price you pay for success.

Momentum

Fast-forward to October 2023.

My phone rang. It was Marshall Haas, and he had big news. Marshall is a good friend and was the majority owner of Somewhere.com. At the time, I was a minority partner, and I owned 12.75 percent of the company. The business was growing exceptionally fast.

I learned of Somewhere.com when I used it to hire my first employee from the Philippines. When that worked out well, I hired a few more folks, and now I've used the company to hire about 80 percent of the employees across my portfolio. It's not an exaggeration to say that overseas labor changed my entire world.

That's because you can get the same fundamental talent for 80 percent less than U.S. wages.

I bought in as a minority investor in April 2022 when the company was very small (less than $2 million of annual revenue), but by October 2023 it had grown to more than 150 employees and *$700,000 of monthly profit*.

Marshall was calling to tell me he had gotten an offer to sell 51 percent of the company at a $47 million valuation. "I want to take the deal," he said. "Do you want to sell half your shares?"

Let's pause for a second.

It's been more than a decade since I hauled boxes at Cornell and elsewhere, but I've continued to take on new, better opportunities.

I'd acquired more than sixty self-storage facilities and employed forty-seven people at my real estate company. I'd co-founded and built a real estate engineering firm (RE Cost Seg) to more than $2 million in annual earnings. I'd taken on a lot of other challenges and failed at many and learned a lot.

Marshall's business was one of the best companies I had ever seen. Somewhere provided exceptional value to clients in the United States and was profitable. It had also *tripled* in size over the previous twelve months.

Now I had an opportunity to sell half my ownership stake in the business for $3 million cash.

What would you have done? Would you have sold down your ownership and taken the life-changing money?

I truly thought there was a chance the business could become a

$500 million revenue company over time and make it to the stock exchange. But if Marshall decided to sell, I would get dragged along and be forced to sell 51 percent of my equity as well.

So I surprised him:

"I don't want to sell any of my shares, and I would like to be the one to buy the company from you at that price."

There were several seconds of silence. He was in shock.

He then asked a lot of questions. How would I raise the $20 million? Would I use a bank? How would I run the company after the transition?

Over the next three months, I negotiated the largest deal of my life.

The buyer who brought the $47 million offer to Marshall was the billionaire and legendary investor Andrew Wilkinson. So first I had to convince Marshall to take my offer over his. On top of that, the company needed a CEO because Marshall would be stepping down. As a result, I had to recruit and hire a new CEO before I even owned the company because the busy season was fast approaching. I couldn't risk a dip in productivity during the summer months. Finally, I had to raise $20 million to make the deal happen and do it in a way where I had some upside.

I worked directly with a law firm to draft and negotiate the purchase agreement, a seller note between Marshall and me, the restated operating agreement, and the rest of the essential documents.

It all came together over a five-month period. I recruited and hired a CEO who started on April 1. In the meantime, profit increased, so the purchase valuation was renegotiated to $52 million. I negotiated an 18 percent seller note directly to me for $9.36 million, which Marshall lent me with shares of the company as collateral. I raised $20.8 million to acquire another 39.25 percent of the business in a private equity tranche.

All in all, I took seventy-five meetings and closed the deal with thirty-eight investors and an average check size of $547,368. It was hard. And stressful. I had to figure it all out as I went. But in the end, I had 70 percent of the voting shares and complete control of the business.

If things go well, it will be a very good deal for me.

The lesson:

Business is all about momentum.

In my first year in business I was driving trucks and moving boxes up staircases. I ended the year with about $15 per hour in earnings.

In my fifth year in business we built a storage facility from the ground up for $2.9 million that is now worth more than $10 million and has made me and my partner double-digit millions each.

In my tenth year in business I acquired $50 million worth of self-storage and raised more than $17 million from investors.

In my eleventh year I co-founded RE Cost Seg, which is on its way to becoming a very large real estate services firm.

And, finally, in my twelfth year in business I negotiated the purchase of a $52 million company. Over the course of forty-one days, I raised $20 million and recruited and hired an executive team to run the company.

If you had told me in 2012 where I was headed, I would never have believed you. And if I could look into the future now, I might be less shocked, but I'd still be surprised by the opportunities, relationships, and money that I plan to acquire during the next few decades.

The point is this:

If you play this game well, the opportunities come at you faster and get larger in scale. They get more exciting. They get more stressful. The stakes get higher. But they get better and better and more fun to chase.

You can handle it.

After a year, you will be much better situated to take advantage of new opportunities than you were on day one. After two years, your leverage will have increased even further. After three years, you'll have new skills. And after four years, your network will start to open up new doors. The sky's the limit from there. It is all about getting in the game and moving quickly. Taking chances. Getting uncomfortable. And seizing opportunities when they present themselves, whether you are ready for them or not.

Start Now

Many people make the mistake of planning and thinking about how they would run a massive company at the beginning. Dreaming about that $52 million deal.

They work on an advanced business plan. Or they decide they have to talk to their customers, survey them, and build a full-on marketing plan before they can do anything at all.

I'm here to tell you that is bullshit.

Your job is to collect the money. Period.

So here's your assignment:

Go out and figure out how to make $500 *this weekend*.

Collect a deposit. Sell a service. Get somebody to hand you cash or send it to your bank account. Convince them to give you their money in exchange for your work. Go get sweaty.

Here is a rule I live by when it comes to entrepreneurship:

Unless you are already wealthy, your first business needs to be making money right away. Therefore, you have to ask for money *immediately*. And if people refuse to give it to you, your idea sucks. People don't actually need what you're offering or they don't trust you to deliver it. There are very few exceptions to this rule. If you can't get money, you aren't solving a problem. You need to go back to the drawing board.

Start small. Start boring. Mow grass. Move something. Clean something. Make it a full-speed race to make $500 in profit.

That's it. That's the beginning. Then you just have to put one foot in front of the other for five years and watch the opportunities grow.

Chapter 3

Not All Businesses Are Created Equal

Let's start by being honest with ourselves about one very inconvenient truth:

Being an entrepreneur is not about you.

The market doesn't care about you or your desires. It doesn't care about what you love doing or what you are good at. It doesn't care about your interests or what excites you. It could care less about what you are passionate about.

If you approach entrepreneurship in a selfish way, you will fail. You'll make poor decisions with a clouded head. Logic will evade you. You'll chase the wrong thing for too long because you "love" it. You'll try to bend the world to your liking instead of accepting things the way they are.

Entrepreneurship is about logic and truth. Successful entrepreneurs accept this fact above all else. Winners understand that there are good businesses and bad businesses. I know because I have done both.

During the ten years I was building and running Storage Squad, I made $150,000 per year. That may sound like a lot for a guy in his twenties, but I worked like a dog. My customers were broke college students. I was learning on the job. I made a lot of mistakes and spent most of my time and energy putting out fires. I ended up selling the business and making about $750,000, which bumped my annual salary during that decade up to $225,000 a year.

About five years into running Storage Squad, my partner and I decided to go into the commercial real estate business. We spent two years building a self-storage facility from the ground up. That project took up about 20 percent of my time while Storage Squad took up the other 80 percent. For the self-storage facility, we were renting out closets with metal doors and steel walls. I didn't have to rent trucks. I didn't have to hire thirty college students per location. We just answered the phones, took credit cards, and kept the place clean.

We built it for $2.9 million and it's worth $10 million today. I still own 50 percent of it, and my business partner owns the other half. We bought out our initial investors. I've personally made multiple seven figures from this one property. So let's do the analysis. Self-storage or a moving company? Which one is fundamentally a better business?

Self-storage. Hands down. No-brainer.

It required way less energy and stress and generated way more profit and value. Probably 10 percent of the stress and ten times more money for each hour invested.

Sure, I needed to convince a bank to lend me seven figures. I needed to convince investors to invest more than $400,000. I had to take the risk of building a building, a project that could have ended in bankruptcy. But by the time I started, I had spent five years honing my skills in a hard business so I could eventually seize the opportunity of a good business.

It takes time and experience plus those three things I discussed earlier—network, operational skill, and capital—to operate at a high level and be able to get into good businesses. You often have to start a hard business and acquire the skills and capital to then advance into a better business. So let's dive into what makes a business feasible and what opportunities I think you should ignore altogether.

The Not-Feasible Business

First things first.

There is an entire category of businesses I would throw out the window right away based on three criteria. Here they are:

Criterion 1: You need to raise venture capital to start said business.

Criterion 2: You have a new idea, and the model does not exist today.

Criterion 3: The model involves manufacturing and selling a physical product.

If you do not have experience running a company and you are not already wealthy, I personally believe these opportunities are a horrible place to start.

Why?

They are highly competitive and difficult. The new-idea method with venture capital is phenomenally hard because it has never been done before. That is a good enough reason for me to look in the other direction. I want a proven model with existing businesses that I can study.

For an inexperienced and undercapitalized founder, the odds of success in these three areas are just way too low. The total failure rate is too high. New ideas don't exist for a reason:

They are hard.

New products are insanely capital intensive and very difficult to bootstrap and turn into profitable companies. These businesses are not realistic for 99.99 percent of humans to go after, because they do not have the skill, network, and capital to make them succeed.

Your goal, remember, is to maximize your chances of earning $30,000 per month while having freedom. No new ideas or products until this is achieved.

How Fun Is This Business?

If your answer to this question is "very fun," forget it.

Remember, you are an opportunist. The less fun a business is, the more money there is to be made. You don't care what is fun or not fun. Eventually, you'll be managing employees and running the business anyway. You don't care if it is picking up garbage or painting houses in hundred-degree heat. The harder the better.

The idea of a restaurant is fun. A lot of people love food, so they open restaurants. But in reality profit margins are slim, and the odds of success are notoriously low. As many as 90 percent of restaurants eventually fail.

Same goes for passion projects. *Are a lot of people passionate about the field you are working on?* You don't want a whole bunch of dreamers in your competition pool. The more passionate people are, the longer they will run a business that isn't feasible. They will lose money and not even care. I don't like competing with people who think with their hearts.

A lot of people are passionate about fitness. A lot of people have tried to start fitness apps. That is why there are thousands of them in the App Store right now that nobody uses.

Is your business in the gaming industry? The health industry? The sports industry?

The odds are it is highly competitive and most people don't make much money. This is just a supply-and-demand equation. The higher the supply of entrepreneurs, the harder it is to find overwhelming demand for your services.

A note:

Some people are very well positioned to chase businesses in some of these "fun" categories. They have experience managing restaurants. They know how hospitality works. They have a vast network in the sports or gaming industry. Their ideas might work in those cases.

But if you don't have a competitive advantage here, ignore these opportunities.

How Much Status Is Associated with Your Business Idea?

You want a business with low status.

You want a business that isn't sexy, exciting, or even a little bit interesting. You don't care what people think about you, and you don't care what people think about your business idea. I'll give you a few scenarios:

Scenario 1: "Nick runs an artificial intelligence business."
Wow! Boo!

Scenario 2: "Nick invented a product he is manufacturing." High profile! Terrible.

Scenario 3: "Nick cuts grass." Boring. I like it.

Scenario 4: "Nick stores people's junk." Perfect.

If you need to status test your business, try this. Go to your grandma (or any older adult) and tell them what you have in mind. If they say, "Wow, that is such a good idea!" it means it is actually a terrible idea and highly competitive and nobody has won that game before.

If they say, "Oh, good for you," that means your business is boring and has been done before and your odds of success are much higher. Don't forget. You *want* a business with low status because this will attract less competition. The dreamers will steer clear.

People watch too much *Shark Tank* and think too much about entrepreneurship through a new-idea lens. This makes them delusional. If no one has succeeded before or if your business doesn't exist yet, it is because nobody has been able to win the game and make money doing what you want to be doing. And if nobody has won, why would you want to play that game?

Competition, Profitability, Odds of Success

To analyze a business model further, we ask three questions:

- How strong is the competition?
- What are the profit margins, industry-wide, in a given business?
- What percentage of people who try to start a business in this field end up succeeding?

Then you do the math. A business that has strong competition plus low profit margin plus high amount of failure equals bad business. For example, an app startup. If you want to build an app, your competition will be Stanford graduates with millions in venture capital. The margins are nonexistent for the first several years. And 99.9 percent of apps die before they make a single dollar.

This is a bad business.

You're looking for a different sort of equation. Unsophisticated and/or weak competition plus high profit margin plus low failure rate equals good business. For example, a self-storage facility. Much of your competition comes from contractors, farmers, people without websites, and folks without college degrees who don't answer their phones. The profit margins, industry-wide, are about 60 percent. I know all this because we operate sixty-eight self-storage facilities at about a 40 percent expense ratio today—60 percent of our revenue is net operating income. And I've never seen a bankrupt self-storage facility. Not one.

This is a good business.

A note:

All of this is region dependent. There are great operators in certain cities and a shortage of companies in others.

A few more examples of good and bad businesses:

- An HVAC company has relatively unsophisticated operators in many markets. It has reasonable profit margins around 20 to 30 percent at scale. Very few of them end up going under. This is a big pie with a lot of demand and a good business.
- A landscaping/hardscaping business has unsophisticated owners. Many don't have websites. Many don't spend money

on marketing. Many don't work hard enough to recruit and hire employees. It is a mom-and-pop-dominated industry. Yet there are fifteen of them in my small town that make more than $100,000 in profit. There are hundreds of thousands of them in the United States that make a good living for their owners. This is a large industry and a large pie. Relatively few of them fail. This is a decent business you can bootstrap with very little up-front investment.

- A software startup has well-capitalized, sophisticated operators. Venture capital funding means it can operate without a profit for years. It has negative profit margins until it reaches maturity. And most people who try new software startups fail. This, in my opinion, is a bad business for the average person.
- A dog-walking app is a target for dreamers. People who love pets and have too much time on their hands. People who code as a hobby. Marketplaces in general are very hard because you are solving for two sides of an equation—customers and providers. You need people to come in and pay for dog walking. And you need people to walk the dogs. Without one or the other, the whole operation fails. Too much of one and not enough of the other, and it fails. In my opinion a marketplace like this is a brutal business and *not* a good opportunity.

The Blue Ocean Strategy

Another common misconception is that entrepreneurs should pursue the blue ocean strategy, an idea popularized in one of the best-selling entrepreneurship books of the past twenty years. Essentially, the blue ocean strategy says that the path to success involves creating a new market where competition does not exist and is therefore irrelevant. According to the authors, Renée Mauborgne and W. Chan Kim, you should expand your offering to new areas through innovation, and then you can have all of the market share.

They caution against pursuing any opportunity in the red ocean, a concept that represents all of the current industries in the economy where competition exists, and the rules of competition apply. The ocean is red because it is shark-eat-shark to compete for food.

I see things differently.

I'd rather start a business in a red ocean. I can study the market. I can pick and choose the opportunities I want to pursue. I can assess the way things are done and figure out if I can compete or have a competitive advantage of some kind. I can learn from my competition.

Most people will read this and gasp.

Nick, entrepreneurship is supposed to be cutting edge! In the red ocean, companies are in a fierce competition for customers! It's a race to the bottom!

But that couldn't be more wrong. A lot of companies are horrifically bad at answering the phone and doing what they say they're going to do. Many don't have a website. Many use a fax machine in their offices and still make millions of dollars in profit per year.

Don't believe me?

Call around for home service companies to come do work at your house. Ask them to build a deck or remodel your kitchen. One in five will answer the phone. One in twenty will have enough time to put you on their schedule. There is a massive shortage of these old-school businesses. The competition is weak. Most do not spend money on marketing. The owners are resistant to change.

Go after an existing market so you can be certain that opportunity exists and there is money to be made.

The Path of Least Resistance

Too many entrepreneurs are gluttons for punishment.

They love the idea of doing hard things. They imagine that being an entrepreneur is like being a gladiator in an arena fighting to the death against all odds. Or the movie *Rudy* where the kid makes the team at Notre Dame against all odds. Or any other story that ends in glory against all odds.

They love terrible odds. That is all bullshit.

Business is a series of games, and some games are easier to win than others.

Think about it like this:

You are playing a one-on-one basketball game against another human and $30,000 per month every month is on the line for the winner. You get a choice:

Do you want to play against LeBron James or a fifth-grade girl?

The winner gets $30,000 per month every month.

I don't know about you, but I'd personally pick the fifth-grade girl every time. This isn't a "see who can do the hardest thing" competition.

Remember something important:

The degree of difficulty doesn't count. We're not doing an Olympic gymnastics routine. There aren't more points for accomplishing something really hard. In business, you can get paid really well for doing easy things over and over again, but you can also get paid zero for doing certain hard things really well. Business isn't a David Goggins ultra-endurance workout.

Trying to start the next Tesla or Facebook is like playing against LeBron James. Starting a self-storage company is playing against the fifth-grade girl.

So what should you do?

Copy what is working. Do what normal people have succeeded at. Find an area where the competition is relatively weak. Find an area where relatively average people succeed more often than not. Where six out of ten or seven out of ten businesses make money and the founders aren't spectacularly smart.

There will always be people who think that stronger competition means a bigger potential reward. And sometimes it does. But they are forgetting the odds of success and the weighted value of taking that chance. A 70 percent chance at $30,000 per month of profit versus 0.5 percent chance of a $50 million exit.

The 70 percent chance at $30,000 is a better deal to take. By far.

They'll be convinced that being an entrepreneur is getting $5 million for beating LeBron versus $50,000 for beating the fifth-grade girl. They'll think taking moon shots is the way to go because of that 0.1 percent chance they build a billion-dollar company.

I used to think this, too.

I studied the tech titans who succeeded against all odds—Musk, Zuck, Gates, Jobs. For a while I wanted to be them. Now I know better. I've met incredibly rich folks without college degrees who don't know how to "reply all" to an email. It's not so complicated. All they had to do was pick the right game to play with the best odds of success, and so can you.

A note:

Even if you aren't an entrepreneur, this applies to your career as well. Some games are easier to win and the reward is more certain. Play those games!

Think Like an Entrepreneur

I have a challenge for you this week. A challenge that will help you radically shift your mindset and think about business and opportunity in a whole new way.

Go for a walk by yourself or with a friend in your local downtown area. Every business you pass by, ask yourself these seven questions:

1. How does this business make money?
2. Roughly how much money do they make per day, week, and month?
3. How many employees do they have, and what do these employees cost the business each month?
4. How much did it cost to start this business? What's the minimum amount of money you would need to make it happen?
5. How much rent do they pay for this location, or how much was it to buy this building?
6. How much profit might this business generate for the owner each year?
7. How much headache does the owner deal with, and what is their day-to-day schedule like?

Observe all of the companies around you. Restaurants, bars, coffee shops, retail stores, professional services, banks, hotels, movie theaters, barbershops, and so on. Get out a napkin and estimate the daily or weekly revenue. Also add up the daily or weekly expenses.

If they are in business in your town and they have been there for a while, they are making money and providing value. Then answer the following three questions:

1. How would I run this business more efficiently if I were the owner?
2. How would I create more revenue or reduce costs?
3. What could I do to make this business just a little bit better? What technology could I use, or how could I find a better way to do things?

I call this a mindset of "business curiosity."

If you look at the world through this lens, you'll begin to discover an infinite number of opportunities. You will start to understand which businesses are good businesses. The ones that are profitable, easy to operate, sustainable, and simple. They lead to a good quality of life for the owners. Either they have enough profit to hire a management team, or they'll be able to sustain the business over time with a steady workforce.

You'll also begin to see which businesses are bad businesses. The ones that are painful for the owners, low margin, and high turnover. Or complex with a lot of moving parts. Most important, you will begin to recognize patterns. You will learn where you might want to spend your time and which opportunities you might want to pursue.

A good practice is to find friends who share this mindset. Take notes on the businesses that stood out to you that week and bounce ideas off them on the phone or over beers after work. It really helps to have someone you trust to bring up ideas you might not have considered.

This is how entrepreneurs think. Their minds are always working to analyze opportunities and business models. Train yourself to think like an entrepreneur.

I do this everywhere I go. I do it with both in-person and internet businesses. I do it with friends and family members, and it starts great discussions on business and operations. It's how I find my own opportunities, and it's how you can uncover yours.

The most common question I get in response to this exercise is this:

Nick, why does it have to be in person? What if I want to start an online business?

A few reasons.

The main one is that everyone who is excited about entrepreneurship and reading books like this wants to start an online business. The competition is fierce! Everyone loves the idea of being able to work from anywhere, sell to anyone, and achieve unlimited scale. And let me put it out there that I don't mind online businesses. I own a few myself.

But the thing about online businesses is that your competition is worldwide. There are no "geographic" moats as there are in local service companies. Somebody in Asia, where the cost of living is 80 percent lower than the United States, can compete with you. The world is flat.

In a real-world business you can pick and choose where you want to compete. You can analyze your local market. There are barriers to entry, and only somebody in your town can decide to compete with you.

The truth:

Not enough entrepreneurs are willing to look up from their computer screens at the world around them. Their own town. Their own local market they can study and analyze.

Close your computer and open your eyes!

Chapter 4

Idea Generation 101

What business idea will you choose? What company are you going to start? Let's talk through how to assess potential businesses using a tactical approach to picking an idea and analyzing the quality of the opportunity. In order to build a healthy company, either you need to pick a market with so much demand you can carve out your own piece of the pie, or you need a competitive advantage. I prefer both.

What is a competitive advantage?

A competitive advantage is how you position your service offering to make customers pick *you*. That means you need to be cheaper, faster, or better than the alternatives. It looks like this:

Price: You charge less money than the competition.

Speed: You have a faster turnaround time than the competition.
Quality: You do the best work.

In order to build a company customers want to spend money with, you have to have an advantage in one of these areas. The value has to be there for the customer.

Considering this, the goal is to look for holes in the marketplace so you can find a way to carve out customers and earn business.

Can I beat the competition on price? Can I show up faster than the competition? Can I do better work than the competition?

Reminder:

You can rarely win in all three areas and you shouldn't try. You need to pick two of the three factors where you want to compete.

If you want to offer the lowest price on the quickest timeline, you may have to compromise on quality. If you want to offer great service at a low price, you'll surely be booked out for weeks and unable to do jobs for customers who are in a hurry. And if you want to do high-quality work for people who want it faster, you'll need to charge more money. I've found that customers are willing to pay more money for fast, great work. Not every customer, but the customers you need to find are those who will pay more to get what they want when they want it.

Warning:

This is the only tactical chapter in the book. I will make you do homework. I will ask you to build a list of business ideas and evaluate them through the lens of price, speed, and quality in order to spot holes in the market where you can compete and win business. If you are more interested in ideas, concepts, and stories, skip ahead to chapter 5.

Reminder:

I'm assuming a few things here.

You are reading a book about getting rich. In this exercise I'm assuming that you aren't rich yet and that is why you are here. I'm also assuming that your time and money are in short supply. They are your most precious resources, so I'm going to show you how to do this while risking as little money and time as you can. You should bootstrap something in a way that won't end in financial disaster even if it goes terribly wrong. We're also going to move quickly so we can learn as fast as possible if the opportunity is indeed a long-term, viable option. Time is of the essence.

But before you build your list of ten business ideas to analyze and potentially start, you'll need to assess your personal situation.

Your Situation and Your Personal Requirements

In the first chapter, you settled on a number that met your definition of financial success.

Now your goal is to build a list of ten businesses you could start based on your situation and personal requirements.

Here are the questions you need to ask yourself to figure out what businesses are feasible for you. These are nuanced questions. There are no black-and-white answers. They are considerations you should make when planning your attack.

How Quickly Do I Need Money Coming In and Do I Need to Keep My Day Job?

Do I have a house payment, kids, car payments, and bills to pay? Or am I fresh out of college on my parents' health-care plan with a free room in their house? Do I need to start my business on nights and weekends while keeping my W-2?

In my case, I started my first company during college when I had zero earning requirements. I had no job. I could afford to make mistakes and go longer without bringing in a lot of money. I was lucky. If I were starting now with three kids and a house payment, my calculus would be very, very different.

How Much Capital Am I Willing to Invest? Can I Afford to Lose It?

Do I have $100,000 set aside I could afford to lose, or do I have $500 in my checking account? How much cash is reasonable to put at risk?

Different businesses require different levels of investment. What are you comfortable with? I have a friend who bought a tree-trimming franchise and had to invest more than $300,000 in equipment to get his operation up and running. He bought a single truck with a boom on it for $90,000 to outfit his first crew.

When I started my moving and storage company, we had no money. We picked up boxes in our cars the first year and used the profit from that first season to buy a cargo van for $1,500 on Craigslist. We slowly invested and grew from there.

What Is Unique About My Town or Location?

Is my town a destination for tourism? Is my town growing in certain areas? Are there a lot of wealthy people in my town? Is there an event in my town that draws a specific type of person?

I have a buddy who lives in Augusta, Georgia. His city hosts the Masters golf tournament every April. He has a side business where he brokers house rentals that month to corporations. His friends in town who own homes pay him money to find them tenants to lease their houses for the week, and he takes about 20 percent. He makes about $50,000 on the side working for one month a year.

What Business Would I Have a Competitive Advantage Starting, if Any?

Do I have any connections or relationships that could lead to opportunity? Do I have any unique skills?

A friend of mine started her travel agency after seeing a massive opportunity at her day-to-day job. The company she worked for planned corporate retreats and company getaways, but many of the executives at the companies she worked for began to ask for similar services for their private travel. My friend ended up starting her own high-end travel agency, and she does really well. She gets paid a 10 percent fee plus another 10 to 20 percent kickback from hotels and resorts to plan $50,000 to $100,000 vacations for wealthy people in her town.

• • •

Use the questions above to assess your current situation. What problem are you positioned to attack? What opportunities are out there? I know it is nuanced and there are no clear-cut answers. But keep your competitive advantages in mind as we move on to the heart of the exercise.

Build Your List of Ten Potential Businesses

It's time to make your list of potential businesses.

And I have a resource for you.

Go to **sweatystartup.com/ideas** to download my list of more than two hundred business ideas. They generally fit the criteria of businesses I like—low risk, not fun, sweaty, in demand. Browse this list and consider adding the ideas you've developed in your own day-to-day life.

There are levels to this game. When we build our list of ten, we're going to consider relatively low-skilled and cheap businesses to start, which I call Level 1. Then, we're going to add a few businesses that are a bit harder and more specialized but still approachable for most of you, which I call Level 2. And last we're going to add a couple of higher-skilled, more capital-intensive businesses, which I call Level 3 businesses.

Let's define each of them:

Level 1 Opportunities

If you have very few skills, no experience running a business, and very little capital, this is your wheelhouse. Your target business should be approachable. No expensive equipment that isn't easy to resell. No advanced training. Your goal here is to go after something very low risk. If you fail, you are fine.

We are going to add five businesses to our list from Level 1. **Your five businesses might include the following:**

- Lawn mowing
- Cleaning services
- Photography
- Mobile bartending
- Car detailing
- Power washing

- Deck staining
- Window cleaning

You will hear people say these are commodity services and that starting one of these businesses is a race to the bottom. This is simply not true. It is only a race to the bottom if you try to compete on price. Instead, you will assess the market to see if you can compete on speed and quality.

My own first business was a Level 1 business—lawn care.

I already owned a pickup truck, and my family had a lawn mower. So I started mowing lawns around town. By the time I went off to college, I had about twenty commercial properties that I mowed each week. I did about $50,000 a year of revenue and $40,000 of it was profit.

There is an eighteen-year-old high school student in my neighborhood who launched a mobile car-detailing business. He bought about $300 worth of supplies and started cleaning people's cars. He now has an employee who helps him, and they do three to five cars per week, making about $50,000 in annual revenue.

I met a college student at the University of Georgia who started her own photography business for corporate events, graduation parties, family reunions, sporting events, and college formals. She charges $500 per event and gets paid nearly $100 per hour for her time. She has one photo editor who works with her in the Philippines who she pays $1,200 per month to help her with all of her editing. It is a great side business!

Level 1 businesses are low risk, and you start by trading your time for money. Without any serious investment, you can do the work yourself and get paid for it! Then you can slowly hire people around you to grow the business as opportunity presents itself.

Don't assume a Level 1 business has zero growth potential. Many of these very small businesses can evolve from single-person startups to large enterprises over the course of five or ten years. You still have the possibility of building long-term value if you operate them correctly and work smart. These businesses will also uncover additional opportunities down the road. For example, your window-cleaning business might expand to window installations or home inspection if the right opportunity presents itself.

My moving and storage company was a Level 1 business, but it opened the door to get into commercial real estate. And the real estate business has generated the majority of my wealth today.

Level 2 Opportunities

These businesses are a bit harder than Level 1 businesses. You have some skills and a bit of experience. You have some capital to invest, say $5,000 to $20,000, and some money saved up so you don't need to be profitable on day one. You might live in a town that lends itself to something niche or you might have some experience running companies or offering a specialty service. Either way, you're ready to explore something that's a bit more difficult for a random Joe to start.

We are going to add three businesses to our list from Level 2. **Your three businesses might include:**

- Niche videography
- Wedding DJ
- Restaurant floor and kitchen cleaning
- Mobile pet grooming
- Airbnb property management

- On-demand holiday decorations
- Beer line/keg cleaning and maintenance

These businesses will generally be a bit less competitive because the barriers to entry are slightly higher. Not just anybody off the street with a Facebook Marketplace ad or a yard sign can service customers. The larger your city is, the more specific you can get. Remember, if you are charging a lot of money to a few specific customers who want the best service on a fast timeline, you can build a business. In some of these industries, you can create a viable business that delivers your $30,000 per month with as few as ten customers.

I know a lady in Bloomington, Indiana, a college town with a big sports scene. She manages about ten short-term rentals and runs two cleaning crews. She gets paid 25 percent of the revenue from the rentals to manage the properties, schedule the maintenance (paid for by the owner), and clean the properties between guests. She also built a cleaning company on the back of her property management business and clears more than $100,000 per year herself with a single admin employee plus her two cleaning crews. That is serious money! She is likely a few years of growth away from her "wealth number."

I have another friend who runs a wedding DJ business. He has three people who work for him in three different cities. Each crew has about $8,000 worth of his equipment (MacBook, JBL speakers, cords, lights, mixers, and so on). To drive business, he has a website and Google Business location with reviews in each city. Each of his employees does one wedding a week throughout the year, and my friend makes about $150,000 on top of his full-time job as a real estate agent. It is a great side business and will generate long-term wealth for him as he invests the proceeds into real estate.

Level 2 businesses are a bit higher risk because they require some up-front investment. Customers are a bit harder to get. Some skill is required. They are a bit more uncomfortable, but the reward and the margins are higher if you operate them well.

Level 3 Opportunities

Level 3 businesses are even more difficult and even more capital intensive than Level 2. For the sake of this exercise, let's assume you have more skills, more cash, and a better network. Even if you do not and are not comfortable taking on one of these more challenging businesses, I still want you to analyze them so you can practice wrapping your mind around a higher-skilled opportunity. For now, let's assume you are willing to take a risk on these businesses to build more value over time.

We are going to add two businesses to our list from Level 3. **Your two businesses might include the following:**

- Dumpster rental business
- Arborist (tree trimming/removal)
- Niche carpentry (decks, offices, wine cellars, sound rooms, home bars)
- Mobile car mechanic
- Surveying

With greater risk in the form of time and capital comes greater potential returns and higher-ticket customers. These businesses might require three years of trade school, five years of experience honing a skill, making a few hires right off the bat, or investing more than $20,000 in equipment or vehicles.

I know an entrepreneur in Athens, Georgia, who started one of these companies several years ago and now has twenty employees, more than 250 dumpsters, and four specialty trucks designed to haul these dumpsters around town. He is handsomely rewarded with more than $750,000 of annual profit coming directly to him.

A while back I met another friend in the tree removal business who bought a franchise for $50,000 and has also acquired $300,000 worth of trucks and specialty tree equipment over time. He took more risk by financing the purchase of the franchise and the equipment through a personal SBA loan. He now runs three crews and manages seven full-time employees, and his business does more than $2 million of annual revenue.

Another guy I know runs a contracting company that builds out new restaurants and gyms. His business does more than $20 million in annual revenue and about $3 million in annual profit. He has a personal net worth of more than $15 million and over $750,000 in his checking account at any given time. He is at a perfect point in his career to go after a Level 3 opportunity in a low-risk way.

This contractor has forty employees, several of them highly skilled project managers. Throughout his time doing the build-outs, he struggled to find spray foam insulation contractors at his North Carolina branch. He knew that if he launched a spray foam business, he could fill up his own schedule and likely get a lot of extra work. So he bought about $75,000 worth of equipment and made two hires without even thinking twice. Within a few months, his crew was busy. He is now planning to hire another crew and continue to invest in this additional business.

These Level 3 businesses require skill. They require a network. They require some capital and experience. But don't let that worry you. If you're not there yet, you will be eventually. And when you do arrive at that moment, you'll be ready because you'll have more experience, capital, and network than you do now.

But back to our list. You now have ten businesses. Five very approachable Level 1 businesses, three slightly more skilled Level 2 businesses, and two Level 3 businesses that would require more investment and more risk.

Let's go ahead and move on to the next phase of the project and narrow it down.

The Ten-Minute Drill

I have a good friend in Athens who I spend a lot of time talking business with when we get together. A few weeks ago we were sitting on my back deck having a beer, and he told me he wanted to start a house painting company.

He laid out the details. The investment in equipment. The prices he could charge. The basic projections. Why he liked the business. Then he asked me what I thought.

"What do you think, Nick? Is painting a good business?"

"It depends. It's a good business in some towns and a crappy business in others. But we can figure this out quickly," I said. "Will you focus on commercial or residential?"

"Residential at first," he said.

It was 6:00 p.m. on a Saturday. I picked up my iPhone. I typed "house painting" into Google Maps, and a few results popped up near me. I called the first one and put the call on speaker so my friend could hear the interaction.

A guy answered on the second ring. I asked him when he was

available to come take a look at painting the exterior of my house along with the fence that enclosed the backyard. He said he could be there tomorrow morning, and if we agreed on the price, he could start the next day. I said I would talk to my wife, thanked him, and hung up.

I went down the list of search results and called three more painting companies. Two of the calls were almost identical to the first one. The owners were hungry for work, and one gentleman even mentioned that he would beat any other price. On the third call, the owner took two minutes, looked at my home on Google Maps, roughly estimated the square footage, and gave me a price of $3,000 for everything.

I had learned enough and so had my friend.

The funny thing about this story is that my friend had been thinking about this idea for weeks. He had done more than ten hours of research on supplies and equipment. He'd bought a web domain and sketched a few potential logos. He had even found a cargo van for sale online and called the guy about it.

But in less than ten minutes we figured out that this business idea, in our town, sucked. All of the competitors were eager to work *quickly* and were competing heavily on price. There were more painting companies hungry for work than there were people with peeling exteriors and messy-looking fences.

The lesson:

Pick up the phone and call your potential competitors. It is unbelievable how few people do this before investing a lot of time and money in a new venture. This takes ten minutes per idea. *Don't skip it.*

Go down your list and do this with all ten of your business ideas.

Google the service. Call the companies. Talk to the owners or the salespeople. Ask them questions to get a feel for how busy they are and how eager they are to earn your business.

Take notes and use your intuition to eliminate six of your business ideas that either aren't realistic for you or are too competitive.

Narrow It Down

You now have your list of four businesses that passed the ten-minute drill, so here is what you're going to do next.

You are going to take it a step further and act like an actual customer. Just like the last step, you are going to search online and contact businesses that provide the services that you are considering offering. But instead of just asking questions on the phone, you are going to get actual quotes for services. This means building a new tab on your spreadsheet for each business idea and listing the ten main competitors in each space. Then you're going to call each company and assess it based on the three factors we've discussed. Price. Speed. Quality.

To assess price, you need to figure out or make a guess at how much the business bills customers per man-hour for the work they provide. If the job takes three people three hours and they charge $900, that is $100 per man-hour.

Getting a price is easy. We got that in three minutes on the phone with the house painting companies. But now, you need to ask the person on the phone two more questions:

How many of your people will come to my house? And how long do you think you will take?

I asked this of a well-drilling company that recently quoted me $8,000 to dig a four-hundred-foot-deep irrigation well at my house.

"Two guys, an eighty-thousand-pound truck, and we will get it done in one day" was his response.

So $8,000 divided by twenty man-hours (two guys working ten hours each including travel) means $400 per hour.

Fill in this dollar figure for each potential competitor. It's okay if you can't quite get all this information from every business you call.

To assess speed, you need to figure out how soon the business could come to your house or be available to do a job. Tomorrow equals fast. Next week equals kinda fast. Next month equals slow. This one is easy. Simply ask them how far out they are scheduling or when they could be available.

The well driller above told me they were scheduling four to six weeks out. Record this on the sheet as well.

Quality is a bit tougher to assess, but I generally judge this as a combination of several things. How good-looking and functional is their website? Can you request a quote online? How kind and professional is their customer service? Do they have good Google reviews and a lot of them? How quick are they to follow up or get you a quote? Do they run digital marketing campaigns? These are all signs that a company is good at running a business and serious about operating the right way.

Record a few data points on each business as columns in your sheet. Google Reviews, Answer Phone, Good Website, Google Ads.

What you're doing is building a matrix to assess supply and demand and determine if there is an opening in the market you can exploit. When you call around to these companies, you are gathering data about a number of things—all of which contribute to the overall strength of your potential competitor. This exercise will tell you a lot about an opportunity in your town.

	GREEN HORIZON LANDSCAPING	ELITE YARD SOLUTIONS	TORRES LAWN SERVICES	TOPNOTCH LAWN CARE	GRASS MASTERS
GOOGLE REVIEWS	4.2	4.7	3.3	5	4.5
ANSWER PHONE	YES	YES	NO	YES	YES
AVAILABILITY	1 DAY	3 DAYS	-	THIS WEEK	TODAY
ESTIMATED TIME	0.50	0.50	-	0.75	0.50
QUOTE	$70	$55	-	$65	$80
# OF EMPLOYEES	3	3	-	2	3
$ PER HOUR	$47	$37	-	$43	$53
GOOD WEBSITE	YES	YES	YES	YES	YES
GOOGLE ADS	YES	NO	NO	NO	YES

I ran this exercise myself and called around for lawn care companies to provide mowing services for my eight-thousand-square-foot yard:

Cost: $37 per man-hour
Availability: can start tomorrow
Online reviews: 4–5 stars

This is a saturated market and a bad opportunity. I don't want to swim in this ocean and compete with a bunch of hungry operators who are very eager to earn the work at $37 per man-hour.

THE SWEATY STARTUP

	PREMIER TREE SPECIALISTS	METRO FORESTRY PROS	MIDWEST ARBOR CARE	TED'S TREE SERVICE	PINE RIDGE TREE CARE
GOOGLE REVIEWS	4.5	5	4.7	3.3	3.9
ANSWER PHONE	YES	YES	NO	YES	NO
AVAILABILITY	3 WEEKS	4 WEEKS	-	2 WEEKS	-
ESTIMATED TIME	2	2	-	2	-
QUOTE	$3000	$2500	-	$2200	-
# OF EMPLOYEES	2	3	-	2	-
$ PER HOUR	$750	$417	-	$550	-
GOOD WEBSITE	YES	YES	NO	NO	YES
GOOGLE ADS	NO	NO	NO	NO	NO

Here is the same exercise with a tree removal service at my house:

Cost: $400+ per man-hour
Availability: available in two weeks
Other notes: No ad spend means the companies are busy!

Tree removal is an expensive business to start and dangerous work. There is also a lot of risk of damaging people's property on certain jobs. But these difficulties make it harder for other competitors as well, and there is clearly more demand in my area than there is supply. The opportunity is there. There's no immediate availability and the cost per man-hour is high.

Got it? Good.

What did you learn? What opportunities on your list stand out? Where do you feel the competition is weak?

With practice you'll start seeing every opportunity this way. You'll also develop an instinct for which businesses will work and which won't *even before* you look at the numbers on a spreadsheet. You'll be able to walk around town and quickly calculate hourly rates and potential profit margins in your head on certain businesses.

Part II
The Skills

Chapter 5

Become an Expert Operator

I recently gave a talk to three hundred entrepreneurs at a conference in Austin, Texas.

I opened with a very simple question. "What is the hardest business in the world? The business that is the most likely to fail? The one that would be the hardest in the world to scale?"

About five people instantly yelled out, "Restaurant!"

I agree. A restaurant would be brutally hard to run, and I do not want to go into the restaurant business. I don't recommend that you go into that business either. But there have been countless restaurants that do very well and even go public.

Texas Roadhouse is my favorite example. It was founded in 1993 as a single restaurant in a mall in southern Indiana. It now operates 627 locations in forty-nine states and 29 international locations in ten countries. It has ninety-one thousand employees. It did $4.7 billion of revenue in 2023 and generated $730 million in profit that year.

It's also one of my favorite restaurants because the food is great and it is an operational marvel. I suggest you go to one (any of them) on a Friday at 6:00 p.m. It will be absolutely packed. There will be more than a hundred employees. And they will do more than $100,000 of revenue *that night*. It is an insanely well-operated company, and it is a *joy* to watch while enjoying a delicious roll, a cheap steak, and a giant $4 beer.

A mom-and-pop restaurant might struggle to make ends meet for a few years and end up going out of business, while another restaurant might go public and scale to billions in revenue. They are in the same business. They are doing the same thing. They are serving food to hungry people in exchange for money.

But there's one thing that separates a great company from a mediocre one—the execution.

You tell me about a hard business, and I'll show you a version of that business that has totally crushed it. Sure, there is timing. Sure, there is luck. But a lot of it comes down to who you hire, how you motivate them, the key decisions you make, and your ability to run a company.

Your idea doesn't determine your success.

It is the execution.

The decisions. The hiring and management. The way business is done on a day-to-day basis. That is what separates the winners from the losers in every area of our economy.

Every Business Is the Same

A lot of people want to start a certain business because they enjoy doing a certain activity. They want to start a web development agency because they enjoy designing websites. They want to open a restaurant because they enjoy preparing food.

Successful entrepreneurs think differently.

> **Cold hard truth:**
> Every single business, when operated at a high level, is fundamentally the same. The owner or CEO is not doing the thing. They are operating the company.

In a well-operated restaurant, the owner is not in the kitchen flipping burgers. In a large web development agency, the CEO is not designing websites. In a tree-trimming business that is making more than $1 million in profit per year, the owner is not in the bucket with a chainsaw.

People start businesses because they care deeply about something or they enjoy a particular activity. And that is fine at the beginning.

But remember this:

Every business, when it reaches a certain size, requires the manager or owner to do the same fundamental things.

You have to sell customers and employees on your vision and your company. You have to solve problems and have uncomfortable conversations about money. You have to hire and fire and manage employees. You have to delegate. You have to outdo your competition on multiple levels. You have to deal with a steady stream of problems and personalities. You can't get rattled every time things go wrong. Because they will go wrong . . . all the time.

That's why operators win in every business model.

Great designers don't build the best design firms. Great landscapers don't build the best landscaping companies. Great plumbers don't build the most profitable plumbing companies.

Great operators do.

Take two car mechanics in the exact same town who each own a repair shop. Same access to customers. Same everything. Put a competent operator in charge of one of them who is average at working on cars. Then in the other shop put a guy who's a phenomenal mechanic but an incompetent operator. No desire to manage employees, sell, stay organized, market to new customers, or hire and fire.

One will do well and one will not. *Can you guess which one?*

The competent operator will thrive while the passionate mechanic will struggle.

Operators are the people who keep their shit together when the going gets tough. They are good at seizing opportunities, decision making, problem solving, closing sales, managing other people, hiring, firing, training, and delegating. You know, all the hard, uncomfortable stuff. The stuff we're talking about in this book.

If your goal is to grow a business, why not focus on learning to operate and be indifferent about what business idea you pursue?

None of this stuff is fun. But excelling at the not-fun, boring, uncomfortable stuff is what separates the successful entrepreneurs from the failures.

Hard things are the key to success. If your life is easy, you aren't going to get anywhere.

It is easy to clock in at work, do the bare minimum, and clock out. It's easy to show up every day and work on cars without talking to anybody else. To go home, drink a beer, play video games, or watch sports. Avoiding uncomfortable situations is natural.

But going to great lengths to avoid discomfort is a surefire way to wake up ten, twenty, or thirty years from now in the same situation you're in right now. No growth. No additional success. Nothing to hang your hat on. No freedom. No security.

Uncomfortable situations forge great business operators.

Stress is relative. For somebody living a soft, easy life, the smallest thing, like a flat tire or a breakdown on the side of the road, can shake up an entire day. But a seasoned, successful, level-headed individual who has grown comfortable with the uncertainty and volatility of life might forget to even mention the flat tire or car trouble at dinner that night.

The more discomfort we face, the better we get at making cool, calm, effective decisions while operating a business. The more comfortable we get in those uncomfortable situations, the more we can accomplish. Every day you get the opportunity to train your mind and build the willpower to handle the challenges life throws at you. It can be humbling and enriching.

It builds immense character.

Want to be successful? Get uncomfortable. Practice the hard stuff over and over. Then watch your world open up.

Build a Franken Business

For several years, I judged college entrepreneurship pitch competitions where students take turns giving five-minute presentations on their new business ideas.

I've since stopped doing this because it pisses me off. They also stopped inviting me back.

Like pretty much everyone else these days, the college kids who enter these competitions think entrepreneurship means reinventing the wheel and flipping a business model on its head. They have little to no experience, yet they proudly announce that they're going to do at least five things totally differently than any company out there. They want to radically change how current companies, making actual money, operate.

It doesn't make any sense!

"Hold on," I'd tell them. "We have an industry that's working and thriving. Companies are providing this product or service right now. They're making money. And instead of changing a few things to make them more efficient, you want to change everything about the way they're doing business? Why?"

Every single student and most of my fellow judges looked at me as if I had three heads when I called out this kind of thinking. They had been trained and manipulated to think they needed moats and differentiators and disruption and scalability.

Their replies were cringeworthy.

I could almost hear them thinking, "Who the hell is this guy? Why the hell would we do something boring and simple like copying others who are winning?"

So they ignored me or pushed back. "That's not what this whole thing is about," one student said. His group was building an app to disrupt the job market and recruiting industry.

"Then what is it about?" I responded.

"It's about thinking of something new and disruptive," he shot back.

"No it isn't." I couldn't help myself. "All that matters is making money and building a sustainable company. Why would you change the recruiting business model? Is making 30 percent of somebody's salary, to the tune of $30,000 to $50,000, not attractive to you?"

My answer didn't go over very well.

When you are starting and growing a business, your job is not to rethink a business model and do twenty things differently. It is to figure out what is working, copy those things, and then do the little things well. The fundamentals. That's it.

I'm not against innovation, but I believe innovation is a long-lost brother of straight up copying what is working. I innovate in my companies all the time, but not in groundbreaking, revolutionary, outside-the-box ways.

I generally copy and steal little things that are working for my other businesses, for my competitors, or for companies in other industries altogether. I take a little bit of this from that operator, put it together with an idea from over here, roll in a marketing method from another player I admire, and voilà!

The result is a franken business made from the best bits and pieces from all of these companies. A franken business might seem like the worst kind—all cobbled together and messy—but that's not the case. Remember you don't get extra points for playing the entrepreneurship game on hard mode. You win by building a boring business based on a proven business model that will allow you to be wealthy, healthy, and free.

When we started Storage Squad, there were already fifteen companies across the country doing exactly what we were doing—student storage over the summer with pickup and delivery.

Big Red was the company in Ithaca, New York, we were competing against, but we knew we could do better. They made a ton of money operating in an insanely archaic way. They took the time to weigh every single box and charged for storage based on weight. Every pickup took well over an hour. They also didn't do last-minute pickups, and they charged for packing supplies.

Guys and Dollies in Bloomington, Indiana, offered free boxes at drop-off points around campus. They scheduled customers for four-hour windows and let them pick a morning or afternoon slot. Most notably, they charged an extra $15 for in-room pickup or delivery. Most students didn't want to pay a premium, so they were happy to bring the items downstairs themselves. That meant they could pick up orders way faster. It was a genius play.

Another company in Boston operating under the UPS Store brand utilized a strategy called hot spots. They set up tables in certain areas of campus during set windows of the day to collect boxes. We borrowed that idea but shrank the "window" down to an exact time. All of a sudden our operations were radically simplified.

We pulled a box truck up to a designated meeting spot in the center of campus, and more than forty customers would be waiting for us with their items. With three guys, we could load an entire twenty-four-foot truck in an hour and bill more than $10,000 worth of storage.

We also instituted "truck swaps" to bring our pickup crews fresh trucks when they filled the ones they were using. We'd have a few drivers on standby running empty trucks from the warehouse to campus and driving back full trucks. This was far more efficient because our drivers and loaders could spend more time doing their actual jobs rather than waiting in traffic or unloading at the warehouse.

One by one, we studied all of the companies across the country and handpicked the best operational strategies from each. And then we built a franken business, bolting on ideas we stole and adapted for our situation.

Very little about our company was new or unique. Actually, almost everything we did was something we stole from a competitor that had already proved it could work.

It didn't matter *at all*.

We charged about the same price as our competitors or even a little less. And our business was more profitable because we were more efficient. We could deliver more storage services per man-hour than our competitors because we were good operators.

Then, once we had a system that worked reasonably well, we started to innovate with a few of our own ideas.

We were the first company to utilize Google Sheets as our scheduling tool so that our employees could use their smartphones to access the schedule rather than a clipboard. This way we could do live updates of the pickup or delivery schedules as new customers booked last-second appointments. We also didn't need to wake up at 5:00 a.m. and print the schedules on-site to get them in the hands of all of our employees.

This was a huge competitive advantage because most companies didn't have an operation that could handle last-second customers. We routinely had a dispatcher put new customers on the schedule just a few minutes before our trucks arrived.

Otherwise, not much about our company was groundbreaking. Our business model wasn't new. Our strategies weren't unique. We simply combined what we saw working out in the open market and built a business that ended up being the biggest and best in the country.

If you've built a list of ten potential businesses, narrowed it down, analyzed the market, and chosen an idea, then you're ready to find customers to pay you so that you can compete against the current competition.

It's go time.

Your job isn't to reinvent the wheel or disrupt a business. The work will be hard enough, so make the rest of it as easy as possible. Look at the companies that are winning, copy what is working, and build a solid business that can carve out a piece of the pie.

The Startup, Sacrifice, and Delayed Gratification

A final word on the mindset of the expert operators who become successful entrepreneurs:

They are great at delaying gratification.

They understand that it is impossible to get it all right now. They are willing to do work today in exchange for rewards four weeks, four months, or four years from now. They understand that it takes sacrifice, boring work, and good decisions compounded for a long time.

Hell, if it were easy, everyone would be running companies and living the dream.

I get some version of this question all the time:

Nick, I'd like to launch a business on the side and go full time when it can cover my bills. But I really value my family time and have kids. I want to be a Little League coach. I want to do family things on the weekends. I go to church every Sunday. I want to be at family dinner, and I want to drop my kids off at school. I want to put them to bed every night. I also really enjoy playing golf on evenings and weekends. Where should I start?

These people have gotten the wrong idea from social media about what it means to be an entrepreneur. They see people touting passive businesses where they need to work only four hours per week to make $500,000 per year! They truly believe that in less than twelve months they can launch a lifestyle business and have perfect work-life balance!

The inconvenient truth is that this is not possible.

If you want to start a side gig on top of a full-time job and maintain work-life balance, you're dreaming. It doesn't work that way. Starting a business is really hard, and you can't give up your main income source until you have a proven model that can feed your family. You will have to make sacrifices. You will miss some dinners. You will miss weekends. You will miss vacations and golf trips.

You are making this sacrifice now for the ability to do *more* of those things in the distant future.

You are delaying gratification.

It all comes down to ambition. *Do you have a real desire to do something very few people are able to do? Do you have the ambition to get wealthy? Are you willing to take chances and invest time in something that might not work?*

Even though it's not the end game, at the beginning you will have to trade your time for money. You will go out there and get paid $50 to $100 per hour to do work for customers. When you have twenty hours a week of that work, and you're making $5,000 per month (or whatever number makes you comfortable), you can quit your job and double down. The bad news? Those hours will have to come from your evenings, mornings, vacation days, and weekends.

If you aren't willing to do this, you should forget about entrepreneurship.

It is unbelievable to me how many first-time entrepreneurs with no money, no skills, and no network think they are going to build a million-dollar business overnight.

They end up failing again and again until they can't support themselves, give up, and go get a job. *Don't let that be you.* Start by trading your free time for money and then slowly build off that foundation. It is less risky. You will learn a ton. Your mistakes won't be as costly, *and* you'll get paid.

Think of an entrepreneurial career as rolling a snowball down a mountain.

At the beginning you have no snowball, but once it starts rolling and picks up speed, things get way easier. The initial accumulation takes time, so the key is to combine patience and momentum. Business is all about momentum, and the beginning is the hardest.

Time has a way of amplifying good decisions and good businesses, so stop thinking about entrepreneurship in a short-term way. Of course you are sprinting at the beginning and keeping the pressure on, but you are really playing the long game.

Do something well for ten years, and it's hard not to be successful. Play a game where most of the people who stick with it end up winning, and it is likely that you will win if you stick with it, too.

Chapter 6

Sales Is the Foundation of Every Business

"Nick, do you like sales? Would you consider yourself a good salesman?"

There I was, sitting across from my mentor Dan Cohen, who I had admired from the first moment we met. He had gotten wealthy off a sweaty startup, working for fifteen years before selling his foundation repair company for high seven figures in 2005.

He was my entrepreneurship professor and mentor at Cornell before moving on to Wake Forest to build a top-shelf entrepreneurship program there.

I had just launched Storage Squad.

I knew from the tone of his voice that I was supposed to say I loved sales. That I went to bed at night thinking about cold-calling and ways to find our next customers. That I thrived on pitching other students on our service. That I didn't take rejection personally.

But instead, after a few seconds of awkward silence and a deep breath, I told him the truth.

"I hate sales. Every interaction is uncomfortable and awkward. I'd rather deal with operations and be the company visionary. I like creating strategy and executing on that strategy."

He rolled his eyes and dropped a bomb that I'll never forget.

"If you don't like sales, I suggest you give up now and go get a regular job. You're wasting your time."

I was shaken.

"Life as an entrepreneur *is* sales," he continued. "You're selling your employees on trusting you and following you. You're selling your partners on coming along for the ride and on what you bring to the table. You're selling your investors on giving you money. Hell, you're selling your vendors on selling to you!"

I had imagined my life as an entrepreneur completely differently. I saw myself in front of a whiteboard strategizing. Or out in the field working on a problem. Or thinking deeply about innovation and growth. Apparently, I had it all wrong. I left his office dejected. He had turned the image I had of running a company on its head, and he hadn't even mentioned selling to customers, which was already killing me.

If every interaction is a sale, I thought, *do I have what it takes to make this company successful? Is he right? Should I go ahead and give up?*

I moped around for weeks afterward, thinking about this exchange. But then I snapped out of it. I started seeing the world in a whole new way. I felt as if I had glimpsed a secret that only wealthy people understood. And I began to accept something as truth:

To succeed in this world, you must have the cooperation of other people.

You need other people to trust you, want to be around you, work for you, buy from you, and more. But this isn't just about business. It's also about relationships, friendships, and how you spend your time.

Anything worth doing in life requires cooperation and interaction with other human beings. From finding a spouse, to having kids who like you, to building a friend group, to creating memories, to making money. It all requires other people.

Another very important fact that you need to accept:

You can't make anyone do anything.

People only do things they want to do. So as a human who wants to be successful in life and business, you have to align incentives to create win-win relationships. Your job is to create situations in which anyone who interacts with you will be better off because of it. *That* is how you get employees to work for you, people to buy from you, people to spend time with you, and more.

Now the most important fact of them all:

Every single person in this world is selfish.

"Selfish" is a strong word, I know. But everyone in this world, including you and me, is looking for ways to make their own life better.

We are looking for friends who bring us joy. For a spouse who is up for adventure, challenges us to grow, and can weather the good, the bad, and the ugly as we build a future together. For an employer who pays well and provides great opportunities. For a business partner who will help us make more money together than we ever could alone.

For most people, the best way to make their lives better is to buy things or to find someone who has the skills, connections, and expertise to solve their problems. People hire surgeons to repair their bodies. They hire companies to repair their homes. They hire mechanics to fix their vehicles. They hire people to build things they need or clean things that are dirty. They pay for tools and services to make their companies more efficient.

That's where you and your sweaty startup come in.

> **Cold hard truth:**
> When it comes to business and sales, it isn't about you.

It isn't about what you want or your problems or what you are good at. *Nobody cares.* They only care about themselves and their own problems.

Entrepreneurs are just as guilty as everyone else of thinking only about themselves. How they want the world to work. What their own goals are. What they want to be doing. When I launched into that conversation with my entrepreneurship professor, I was thinking about business as a vehicle for my own personal fulfillment.

Luckily he smacked some sense into me.

Just like everyone else, entrepreneurs are self-interested. And often we are delusional because everything we do is filtered through our ideas about what we want to be doing and our own problems. We start businesses based on our own interests. We care about what people think of us and our status in the community. We often have a predetermined path we want to follow, and we have a tendency to ignore information that tells us we might be wrong.

But to succeed at sales and life you have to be unselfish and focus your energy on other people.

These are the four fundamental truths of life:

1. You can't do it alone.
2. You can't make people do anything.
3. Everyone in this world is selfish.
4. It isn't about you.

So how do we use these four fundamental truths of life to get what we want?

Sales.

We sell ourselves and our ideas. We convince other people that their lives will be better if they trust us, work for us, buy from us, and more. We make people *want* to do things with us and for us. We make them *want* to pay us money because we are so good at solving their problems. We look at the world through their eyes and try to think like them. We put ourselves in their shoes. We make it all about them.

And by doing that, we sell them *on us*.

I look back on that conversation with my mentor about sales as one of the most important conversations of my life. Because he was 100 percent right.

Shortly after that, I met my future wife, and I sold her on spending the rest of her life with me. I sold my business partner Dan on building companies with me. Eventually, I sold employees on working for me and investors on trusting me with their precious capital. I sold real estate owners on trusting me to pay rent for warehouses. Once I changed my outlook, it was so obvious. As an entrepreneur, I was indeed selling 24/7.

If you want to build a company and become wealthy and successful, you have to get good at sales. Not for yourself, but for other people. Customers need your service. Employees need your wages and opportunity. Partners need your skills or capital. Vendors need to be sure you can pay and hold up your end of the bargain. You are selling what you bring to the table and how you can benefit other people in every single interaction. Luckily I woke up and took this seriously.

In the end, sales changed my life. It can change yours, too.

The Seven Habits of Highly Effective Salespeople

Fifteen years ago, at that meeting with my mentor, I was indeed terrible at sales.

I was scared to death, and everyone knew it. I had no confidence. I didn't feel comfortable asking people to pay me money. I had no charisma in meetings with potential employees.

I am a phenomenal salesperson today. I am confident. I embrace the uncertainty of these interactions. I'm better at building trust.

How did this shift happen?

Practice.

Nobody is a natural-born salesperson. Sure, some people are more extroverted and better communicators than others, but that doesn't happen automatically. And I have good news:

You can become a great salesperson. It is a skill that can be acquired through practice and work.

The most important aspect is confidence. If you can climb the mountain and overcome your fear, you will get better at selling yourself and your business. You will get richer. You will be happier. You will live a more fulfilling life and positively affect more people.

A note before we dive in:

Sales is a self-fulfilling prophecy. If you tell yourself over and over again that you hate sales and that you suck at sales, you will continue to suck at sales. If you tell yourself you are a great salesperson (even if you aren't yet), your confidence will shine through, and you will indeed become a better salesperson.

So let's discuss the seven habits you can implement to improve your sales ability and watch your world open up.

Habit 1: Realize Not Everyone Wants to Buy What You're Selling

You can't trick someone into buying something from you. Some people want what you are offering, and other people don't.

The sales process is about figuring out if you are a good fit for someone, but it also involves vetting other people to see if they are a good fit for you. You are on the lookout for red flags. You are trying to disqualify people who could become a pain in your ass. Ask good questions and interview your counterpart. This builds trust and shifts the dynamic in your favor in subtle ways. You'll come off as less needy. More professional. More trustworthy.

Gimmicks and shady maneuvers won't increase your close percentage. Emotional bullying or manipulation doesn't work when it comes to doing business in today's world. Handing somebody a pen at the right time and moving their hand toward the signature line will make your potential customer run for cover. While that might have worked fifty years ago (I have my doubts), it definitely doesn't work today.

Don't get pushy.

You don't need to do business with anyone and everyone. You don't have to accept assholes as customers or partners. And most of all, you shouldn't ever come into an interaction from a position of desperation.

When I was shopping for engagement rings for my future wife, I had one of these old-school interactions in Elgin, Illinois. I walked into a jeweler and asked about their diamonds and bands. I told them what size diamond I had in mind and that I had a $5,000 budget.

The owner of the shop sat me down and put a great-looking ring in front of me. He showed me the stone under the magnifying glass, told me all kinds of wonderful things about it, and said how it was an absolute steal. Then he did something surprising. He asked his assistant to draw up the receipt. He put a pen in my hand and said, "Sign here."

I got the hell out of there and never went back.

The old-school sales books will not help you advance your ability to sell. The last thing the modern customer wants is a pushy salesperson manipulating them into buying something they don't need.

Don't do this.

You can follow up. You can be persistent. You should follow best practices when it comes to closing deals, but first things first. You shouldn't try to manipulate your prospects.

Habit 2: Get Comfortable Being Uncomfortable

Why do great salespeople make so much money?

It's simple. They can tolerate the discomfort of being rejected.

Ultimately, making the sale comes down to picking up the phone over and over again and not being afraid of rejection . . . because you'll get a lot of it.

Rejection sucks. I've been hung up on more times than I can count when cold-calling self-storage facilities to source deals. I've been laughed at on calls with potential investors. I've had folks tell me we'll never make money and that we should find something else to do.

Get used to it.

Sales is a numbers game, pure and simple. Even if your close rate is 2 out of 1,000, if you make 100 calls a day for 10 days, that is 2 new customers.

The key is consistency. Your job is to cast a wide enough net to find the right people. The people who want to buy from you or work with you or sell to you or invest with you. You sometimes have to go from coffee to coffee, dinner table to dinner table, or Zoom call to Zoom call to find the right match. You have to wake up every day and dedicate time to sales just as you dedicate time to brushing your teeth. Even if you feel uncomfortable at first, even if you dread it, it has to be automatic.

You must embrace the uncomfortable feeling of rejection and try to make the sale happen *anyway*.

My real estate journey started with a world of rejection. I met with more than a hundred investors before I raised the money for my first deal. Many of them laughed at my experience level, my command of the numbers and the industry, and my pitch in general. I also met with more than ten banks that were potential lenders for that first real estate project. They turned me down for myriad reasons, many similar to the reasons the investors turned me down.

You don't have the experience. What makes you think you can build a building from the ground up? How can you operate it? You've never done self-storage before. The real estate market is about to crash. That site you picked is horrible.

We eventually found five people who invested nearly $500,000 and one bank that would lend us $1.7 million. I was twenty-six years old, and I learned a valuable lesson:

With confidence and enough tries, you can sell anything.

But it is hard. My hands would sweat before every meeting. I'd get a lump in my throat. I'd get anxiety. I wouldn't want to walk in the door or pick up the phone or log on to the Zoom call. The fear of rejection is real. It hurts to get told no in person when you are trying to make a big, bold move.

Over time, the investor meetings became more natural. The bankers began to feel my confidence. During employee interviews, I got better at selling people on my vision and persuading them to trust me to guide the ship. That's what it's all about. To master sales, you must smile and be confident, embrace the rejection, and get comfortable being uncomfortable.

Habit 3: Prove That You Are an Expert

How do you show people you have what they need so that you get enough leverage to call the shots?

You have to know your stuff.

That doesn't mean bragging about yourself or talking endlessly about what you've accomplished. Instead, it's about speaking the other person's language. And even though it seems counterintuitive, you can build trust by talking about the risks, difficulties, and potential problems inherent in any deal or project.

Basically, you talk about why business is hard.

Few salespeople do this. The typical approach is to focus on the upside and tell a customer or investor about all the great things and why what you're selling is absolutely perfect. That's never worked for me. Every time I took this route in the early days, I could see it right away:

The potential buyer was on high alert because they were getting a "too good to be true" feeling.

So what does it look like to do exactly the opposite? Let's run through this trust-building exercise using a few examples:

Suppose you're talking to a self-storage owner and trying to buy their property. Rather than going on and on about your net worth or the hardest deal you've ever done, you can quickly tell them you already own eight facilities and speak to them about management software and the other nitty-gritty details of their day-in and day-out business. This immediately separates you from the pack by proving that you are an expert. You are in the game.

Or if you're talking to a potential investor, you speak about risk factors, how you think about the economic environment, and the inherent risks of *this* deal. This puts you on another level from most of the real estate shops simply touting the benefits of buying real estate and how it always goes perfectly.

If you are a web developer, this might mean talking about the pitfalls and security risks of popular web hosting services. Or the challenges business owners face to rise to the top of the Google search results when they're setting up their websites or converting customers with paid ads.

If you're a recruiter, you talk about the land mines or blind spots most hiring managers have when it comes to finding qualified candidates. You tell stories of candidates folks thought would work out *and then* share why they ended up failing and costing the company serious money.

Relating your experience and expertise directly to the wants and needs of the customer shows the other party that you understand the difficulties of the business and the complexities of the market. You've been there. You've dealt with problems and made decisions before. You are an expert. And you're an asset.

They should pay you a lot of money to keep them out of trouble.

Habit 4: Manage Expectations

Stress = unmet expectations.

Show me a stressed-out person and I will show you somebody who overpromised and is having trouble delivering.

A bit of stress while growing a business is natural. Sometimes you need to step up and make a courageous promise to win some work even when you are filled with uncertainty. That is part of this game, but that's no way to run a business day to day.

Instead, let's focus on a great practice that works 99 percent of the time:

Managing expectations.

The best examples I know of to illustrate this point are two of my friends, both of whom run general contracting businesses. They build and remodel people's homes, which is incredibly stressful, difficult work.

My buddy, John, builds about ten custom houses a year and earns well into the seven-figure range. He has seven employees who have been with him for years. He plays golf, rides mountain bikes, travels, has free time to coach his son's baseball team, and is building serious wealth.

Then there's my friend Bill. He builds two houses a year and earns enough to pay his bills and feed his family with some money set aside to live in a nice house and drive a new truck. He is always busy, stressed, and complaining about business when I see him.

These guys are in the same line of work, so how is it possible that one is stressed out all the time and earning a few hundred thousand dollars a year while the other is not stressed at all and earns almost ten times as much money?

Aside from the fact that John is likely a better manager and operator, there is one serious difference between the two.

John is excellent at managing expectations during his sales interactions with clients. If he thinks he can build a house in eight months with perfect weather, he'll tell the customer twelve months. If he thinks the kitchen a client wants will require a $50,000 upcharge, he'll tell them they should budget $60,000. If he thinks the appliances will take six months to be delivered, he'll tell his clients to be prepared to wait nine months.

He'll discuss the ideal scenario, but he also tells clients about the realistic or even worst-case scenario. He'll highlight the difficulties in the construction market *and* the ways he manages costs and timelines. John's customer leaves the conversation knowing they spoke with somebody who knows the business and is a straight shooter. He manages expectations phenomenally well.

On the other hand, Bill is terrible at managing expectations. To make the sale and get a new client, he promises a great price on a tight timeline. He doesn't account for delays or potential problems during the remodel or project. He'll say the appliances will take six months to arrive even though, in his experience, they almost always end up taking longer.

Bill tells the customer exactly what they want to hear. If they ask for a timeline, he'll make impressive claims and promises. He'll spend the entire meeting talking about how good he is and how everything will go perfectly. But his days are actually full of stress. He is constantly fielding calls from unhappy clients or subcontractors. He is always putting out fires because of the expectations he sets for himself.

It doesn't have to be that way!

The truth about expectations:

One difficult conversation at the beginning of a relationship will save you five even more difficult conversations at the end.

You'll get pushback when you deliver the initial news. You might get a sigh or an underhanded comment. You might even get somebody who tells you that it is unacceptable. Good deal. You just saved yourself a lot of headache working with that person who would become a nightmare for you later.

Habit 5: Add Value First

A few years ago another mentor of mine gave me some advice that changed my life.

I had just made my first bit of money, and he was a successful wealth manager and business consultant. He brought me into his office, where he spent ninety minutes with me and my wife getting our full financial picture and putting it up on a whiteboard. He asked questions about our businesses and revenue. Our team and structures. He brought up helpful strategies we should consider. He added a ton of value to our lives and our financial plan in real time.

"Key man insurance would help you here if you or your partner get killed or injured. You should consider bonus depreciation and a cost segregation study on that building you bought. A captive insurance policy for your tenant protection at your storage properties might be highly profitable. You could open an interest-bearing account or do treasury management at this company and make an extra $30,000 a year."

It was one of the most valuable consulting sessions I've ever had. At the end, he took a picture of the whiteboard, emailed the photo, handed me a stack of notes and handouts on each topic, and was about to send me on my way.

"Where's the bill? Send it over and I'll gladly pay you. What do you normally charge people for that kind of session?" I asked.

"I do this for all potential clients. I never charge for the first meeting."

My jaw hit the floor. *Was he kidding?* He had just added hundreds of thousands of dollars of value to my life and he didn't want to charge me?

"So how do you make money?" I said.

"Nick, this world is about adding as much value as possible with no expectation in return. If people trust me, they will want to work with me. Most people walk out of here and sign up on the spot. The ones who don't end up coming back a year later when they have more questions and sign up with me then."

I learned from that moment. And I don't worry about the money on day one. I *first* add as much value as humanly possible, show people I can help, and build their trust. Then the money takes care of itself.

My friend the wealth manager understands this principle better than anyone. He knows that the people who win put others first and solve problems. They make people's lives better and easier with no expectation in return. So he approaches sales in an entirely different way. His clients find it refreshing, get a ton of value from it, and end up feeling great about paying him for his help.

Here's the secret:

You can do this in any business.

I have a friend who is a prominent CPA. He advises very wealthy individuals on their tax strategy. He built a free resource library to educate his customers, typically real estate investors and business owners, on strategies for building wealth and saving money on taxes. He's put together hundreds of pages of PDFs and a book that tells everyone exactly what he knows.

People don't want to hire him? That's fine. They can still read what he knows for free. He also does free consultations where he provides a ton of highly customized, actionable advice to people who are not yet his clients.

Or take my brother. He runs a lawn care business and writes how-to articles sharing his knowledge about different plants and landscaping techniques. These articles attract visitors to his website who want to do things themselves, some of whom, in the end, hire him for his expertise.

Add value -> build trust -> get sales.

Find a way to prove your worth by adding value first and a sale becomes much easier!

Habit 6: Make Scarcity Work for You

Once you've proved that you're an expert, managed expectations, and added value, it's time to gently push your customers away.

You're probably thinking, "What are you talking about, Nick? This is the moment to go in for the kill."

Wrong. Wrong. Wrong.

Instead of pulling them closer and funneling them straight into your sales pitch, you need to talk with your potential customers about all the reasons why you might not be a good fit.

If you're running a service business, that might mean emphasizing that they could probably find a cheaper option out there somewhere because you focus on quality. It might mean letting them know that you are extremely busy and looking for a certain type of customer. It's saying that you're only accepting customers who are willing to sign a one-year contract. Or if you're talking to investors, you might touch on the types of investors your deal *isn't* for or what kinds of facilities *don't* work with your model.

If you've started a boring business with a proven business model, this won't be a lie. You really are focused on quality over cutting costs. You really are busy. Your skills are in high demand. You aren't a perfect fit for everybody.

You're not creating a false sense of scarcity because what you're saying is true. You work with a specific type of person on a reasonable timeline. Not every customer is right for you. Not every investor is right for you. You and your company will not be a match for everyone. That's the deal. Take it or leave it.

But, Nick, what if I really need the work and I'm not actually busy?

Pretend that you are.

This is *very* hard in the beginning. Because you do indeed need the work. You aren't an expert yet. You don't have a lot of experience. Those first sales are the hardest, and they require persistence, guts, and courage.

But it gets easier and easier as time goes on.

And if you're doing it right, you will gradually have more leverage. One day you might think, "I don't want to work with this customer." And you'll realize that because of your skills, network, and capital, you don't have to. The more leverage you get, the more scarcity you can create. And ironically, the larger your business gets, the more customers you can turn away.

Far too many business owners get personally attached to winning every sale. They feel beaten down and depressed if a competitor undercuts their price and they lose a job. This is a horrible mindset.

If you are closing 70 percent of your leads, your pricing is too low. You are stretching too much to win work. Losing jobs is a blessing. Keep your head up and move along. Go find that customer who is willing to pay for what you have to offer and treat you with respect along the way.

There are a lot of really bad customers out there. Customers who will yell at your employees, emotionally abuse you, bully you, leave you a one-star review, and just generally make it their mission to cause problems and make your business lose money.

You don't want these customers. And if you have them, you need to fire them right away. One of the primary objectives of your sales calls is to look for signs and spot these customers.

Generally speaking, I am a proponent of exceptional service and making your customers very happy, but unfortunately some of them do not have your best interest in mind.

Do not do business with these people. Turn them away. The customer is not always right.

Habit 7: Let the Other Party Sell Themselves

At the end of a sales call I like to ask an open-ended question.

If you're talking to a customer, it goes like this:

"This is a tough project with a lot of risks. I think we have a great plan to manage them, but what makes you think I could be a good fit here?"

Or if you're speaking to an investor:

"Given the risks we've discussed, why are you interested in investing in this project?"

Or if you're speaking to a potential web development client:

"Look, I'm busy and it'll take us a few weeks to get on this. I know other companies are likely ready to go sooner. Why do you think I'm the right fit?"

Then it's time to shut up and let your counterpart have the floor.

Because nine times out of ten, an amazing thing happens at this moment. The potential customer starts to talk, and *they begin to sell themselves.*

They tell you why they would make a good customer. How your circles overlap. They soothe themselves when it comes to any concerns or objections, and then voilà! The rest of the conversation goes swimmingly. They've already convinced themselves they want to work with you.

That's because they know you're going to do the hard work. They know you are thinking about the risks. They know you are aware of how hard it is. They also know that you are in high demand and that you are busy for a reason.

In the case of a customer, you've shown that you understand the scope of the project, the timeline, and what it's really going to cost. In the case of an investor, you've demonstrated you're a pessimist, you're conservative, and you're protecting their downside.

People are very surprised when you do this. They let their guard down. *Holy cow, this company is wondering if I would make a good customer? Wow, these people are on another level,* they think to themselves.

It's a virtuous cycle. Letting the other party sell themselves turns the old-school pushy sales dynamic on its head and builds even more trust with your potential customer. Try it and watch your world open up.

Change the Dynamic

Part of the reason I know that these strategies work is that I use them every day. Let's run through a real-life example so you can picture it and apply it to your business.

This is how I frame conversations with potential investors about investing in my real estate deals. Part of the way we've raised more than $50 million of investor capital is because on every call I turn the sales dynamic upside down. It's not that I don't want these people to invest—I absolutely do. My goal is to get the investor to write a check for anywhere from $50,000 to $1 million.

But even more than closing the deal, I want to build trust and make sure they are a good fit and would make a good partner. Here's how I do it:

I open the call and prove that I am an expert.

I explain how I think about storage. Our strategy. How we are operationally superior. Why we're good at what we do. This takes just a few minutes. But instead of keeping that sales-forward dynamic going into the call, I turn it around.

I start discussing the risks and what I'm worried about.

I talk about how real estate is cyclical and how interest rates, which I cannot control, greatly affect the value of properties. I discuss the external factors that affect our ability to secure bank debt or find a buyer for our properties. I say that our projections are not guaranteed.

I spend some time talking about our plan to navigate a tough environment and fight through difficult stretches. How we are preparing and thinking about those risks. How we are very selective about our partners and the storage properties we buy. What I'm doing here is proving that I'm an expert, managing expectations, vetting my counterpart by trying to scare them away, and making scarcity work for me.

Then I drop the bomb.

"Let's discuss a potential scenario. Let's say you invest $100,000 in our next deal and we buy a storage facility. Right after that, interest rates start to go up quickly, self-storage rentals slow down significantly because houses stop selling as frequently, and the property begins to miss projections. Let's say we enter a real estate recession and values are depressed for a long time.

"Unless things got really bad, we wouldn't lose the property, but we can assume we'd miss projections and you wouldn't earn much on your investment for a while. What if our five-year time horizon became ten years and you were stuck with me in an illiquid investment with subpar returns? How would you feel about this?"

Then I shut up.

It's always an awkward moment. You'd think they'd close the computer and run away. Why would they invest with somebody with this mindset? That all sounds scary as hell!

But then something amazing happens.

Most of the time the person on the other end of the video call begins to sell themselves on self-storage and real estate and my business. They counteract my warnings and honesty with all the reasons they still think it is a great investment. *The dynamic shifts.* During the next few minutes of the call, they become the salesperson. It's basically a done deal.

They also really like that I'm not a pushy salesman.

They like that I'm not just constantly bragging on the positives and talking about what could go right. They don't pay me to manage their money and be wildly optimistic. They pay me the big bucks to protect the downside. They *like* that I am aware of the risks and that I worry about them. They want somebody managing their money who worries about the downside!

I also do a version of this when I am interviewing potential employees for management positions at my companies. I spend a little bit of time telling them how excited I am about the vision and how aggressive I am when it comes to growth. I let my charisma and leadership shine through. But then I generally try to scare them away.

I tell them how hard everyone works and that sixty-hour weeks aren't out of the question. I tell them how we have a startup mentality and a lot of change happens fast as we grow. I talk about the differences between our mindset and methods and those of most midsize or large companies. We're more intense.

Then I ask them why they are still interested in the job, and I shut up while the great candidates get even more excited and sell themselves on the job. The people who aren't willing to really get after it generally show themselves too. It is very effective.

Now I have an exercise for you:

I want you to spend some time framing your own sales pitch using this structure. Think about what you are selling and tailor this method to your own business. You might be selling a catering contract, a rollaway dumpster, or a structural engineering job—it doesn't matter.

Work from the framework above:

What should you highlight to prove you are an expert and can be trusted? List three potential risks you worry about *every* time you acquire a customer or do a job. What could go wrong? What do you and your customer need to worry about?

How can you vet your prospects and disqualify the ones who are not a good fit? What makes somebody a good customer or a bad customer?

What questions can you ask to figure out what camp they fall into? How can you add value for your prospect so that even if they don't hire you, they walk away smarter or better off?

How can you manage expectations? What questions are common, and how have you gotten yourself into trouble by overpromising in the past? What can you change?

How do you add an element of scarcity to your offering? Maybe you respectfully and humbly discuss how busy you are or how selective you are about the work you do.

How can you flip the dynamic by asking the right questions so your prospect begins to sell themselves?

Two notes before we move on:

A huge mistake I see people make when it comes to sales—they never record their sales interactions to analyze them afterward.

Pro athletes watch game tape and study plays. Sales is simply running a series of plays. Why wouldn't you review your work so you can adjust? This makes a massive difference and everyone should do this. But few ever do. It is really one of the *only* ways to improve your delivery, responses, and framing over time.

Record yourself. If you do your calls in person or over the phone, buy a $50 digital tape recorder. Put the call on speaker or put it in your pocket for in-person meetings. Use a tool like Fathom to record your online meetings.

Last thing:

You still need to ask for the business. You can't play hard to get when it's time for your prospects to sign the deal or move along.

If you are too afraid to directly try to close a deal, it won't happen. This is another huge mistake many salespeople make. You can't play passive when it comes time for somebody to send you money. Get good at *closing* and asking for the money.

Marketing

Those first sales give you confidence. You've gotten over your fears, you've done some real work and made a little bit of money.

But what then? What happens when you exhaust your network of friends and family? What happens when you've served your first, most obvious customers and then you need to find more? Where do you go and what do you do to get the word out about your business?

That's when it's time to consider guerrilla marketing.

The way people think about marketing (and the way marketing majors are taught marketing) is wild to me. Spending money on ads. Branding. Flashy commercials. Instagram reels. Million-dollar budgets.

That stuff is important for mature companies, but it is totally out of reach for your everyday broke entrepreneur trying to get their first venture off the ground.

> **Cold hard truth:**
> In the early days you must do the things that do not scale. The hard stuff. The common things that work but that most people are unwilling to do because they are difficult.

We didn't spend a dollar on mainstream marketing at my company until 2017, six years after we began. By then, we were doing more than $2 million in annual revenue. It was then, and only then, that we ran our first Google ad and did our first paid promotion on social media.

Instead, we got scrappy.

In the spring of 2013, we paid $2,200 for a ten-year-old, sixteen-foot box truck on the South Side of Chicago. We loaded it with supplies—twenty thousand flyers, forty boxes of sidewalk chalk, tape, T-shirts, and moving boxes. I drove from Chicago to Boston, where my girlfriend, now wife, was doing a clinical rotation at Harvard to become a registered dietitian.

I crashed on her couch for two months and spent eight hours a day sneaking into dorms sliding a flyer under every door. I have personally been in every dorm at MIT, Northeastern, Boston University, Harvard, Tufts, Brandeis, Emerson, and a few others. To this day, I know these campuses in and around Boston like the back of my hand.

We also did the stuff that didn't scale. I got up every day at 6:00 a.m. to write chalk advertisements in high-traffic areas on campus where we knew our customers would walk at 8:00 a.m. Instead of drawing elaborate ads, I simply wrote "Student Storage, StorageSquad.com" over and over and over again. I've written those words more than five thousand times in my life, and when I got going, I could lay down three ads in a minute. I've worn holes in the knees of my jeans many times. I've handed out Popsicles along with coupons for storage in high-traffic areas of campus.

None of it was sexy. Not a single one of these strategies has ever come up in any marketing class . . . ever. None of it was scalable and easy.

But it all worked really well.

Sign-ups began rolling into our inbox faster than I could believe, and by mid-April I had to switch the chalk advertisements to recruiting employees.

"$15 an hour + tips. Flexible schedule. StorageSquad.com/Apply."

That worked, too. We found great employees with these chalk advertisements on all of our campuses over the years.

Through guerrilla marketing, we got our entire business off the ground.

But it's not just us. As I mentioned, my brother runs a lawn care company in Bloomington, Indiana. Every April he buys about a hundred bandit signs—those little signs you stake into the ground near intersections—that read, "Lawn care and weed control. Great prices and quality work." He puts them all around town and replaces them when they're taken down. Do they work? Yes!

More than half his new clients cite the signs as the way they found out about his company.

He uses guerrilla marketing to attract employees, too. He puts up flyers at gas station pumps and advertises $20/hour for lawn care help. He's hired more than five employees that way. No job boards. No LinkedIn recruiting.

I'm a partner in a pest control company that operates under the brand names Spidexx and Bug Shark. We have one main competitive advantage:

Door-to-door sales.

Not scalable. Not flashy. Not sexy. No crazy branding. Just groups of clean-cut, smooth-talking salespeople who go door-to-door with a clipboard asking people to sign up for pest control services. It works wonders. In this day and age, where it feels as if all of life has gone online, a crew of eight to ten salespeople can *still* sell $1 million worth of contracts in one summer and drastically grow a business. It is wild.

The big idea here is that everything you think you know about marketing is not applicable to your small business. The marketing books are wrong. Large social media ad budgets. Flashy branding events. Company swag. Giveaways. Commercials and paid media.

What actually works for small business:

Figuring out where your customers are and getting in front of them in unscalable, common, sweaty ways. I knew exactly where my customers lived and went to class. So I got in front of them in the simplest way possible.

Most people are not willing to do this work. Getting rejected is hard. And getting rejected in person is brutal. People would rather spend more money on Google ads or Facebook ads. They don't like managing teams who go door to door. They don't like putting bandit signs out at 5:00 a.m. They don't like running around campus with sidewalk chalk.

You are not most people. Your competitors aren't willing to do the hard, non-scalable stuff. If they do it, they'll stop it as soon as they get a full schedule or a few more customers than they can handle. Make it a priority. Get comfortable being uncomfortable. If you are willing to do it, you can grow your business beyond your wildest dreams.

Chapter 7

Life Is Short

When it comes to money and a network, every person in the world starts on a different footing. One person might be born to an entrepreneurial family with a successful business. They might grow up around the kitchen table talking about operations, hiring, opportunities, and investing.

It is an incredibly huge advantage to be born into these kinds of circumstances. Having a supportive family and a safety net to fall back on is definitely a big part of success, but having the mindset of an entrepreneur is arguably even more important. My kids are probably ten times more likely than the average kid to become entrepreneurs. They might not choose that route and that's fine, but if they do, they'll likely be successful just because of the culture in our household.

There is one area, however, where everyone is on exactly the same footing and has exactly the same resources.

Time.

Every single human, no matter how effective or successful or broke or disadvantaged, has exactly twenty-four hours in a day. Some people invest wisely and use that twenty-four hours to build wealth. They delay gratification. They do hard things for a potential reward much later. They get comfortable being uncomfortable and develop skills that add value to the world.

Others spend it freely and frivolously and use that twenty-four hours to maximize enjoyment in the moment. They do whatever they feel like doing. They do not plan ahead. They do not take a disciplined approach and build good habits. And as a result, they aren't able to add much value to the world.

Elon Musk has the same twenty-four hours in a day that I do. He has simply invested it more wisely, made better business decisions, and solved harder problems than I did from day one. That is why he is so much more successful in business than I am. But that's okay.

You are the ultimate investor of your most valuable resource. It's the only resource you can't get more of.

How you decide to spend your time, and what decisions you make along the way, will influence your level of success. Move quickly and develop a sense of extreme urgency. Time is of the essence. Make the most of it.

The Scarcity Mindset

In almost all areas of life I have an abundance mindset.

More opportunity for somebody else means more opportunity for me. My friends winning means I'm more likely to win. The more successful people I can be around, the more likely I am to become successful. I firmly believe in sharing freely to create synergies and opportunities. There will always be more money to be made or more opportunity to be created.

But I feel differently about time and you should too.

Why is it that people hoard money and protect every last dollar but give their time away freely and liberally? If your neighbor knocked on your front door and asked you for $100 to go to the local pub and drink beer, what would you say?

No way. Of course not. That is crazy.

But if your neighbor knocked on your door and spent thirty minutes talking your ear off about things you don't care about, what would you do? You'd likely be polite and listen while he burned 35 percent of your family time that day.

Or how about the person who isn't your type, doesn't make you better, and is a drag to spend time with? What do you do when they text you? Or when they ask you to get together? You don't want to be rude. You probably spend time and energy on this person because they ask for it. You feel obligated to give your time away freely.

But why?

Disclaimer:

This is a mental exercise.

I'm not suggesting you refuse to help your neighbor and walk around acting as if you are too good for everybody. I'm suggesting you adjust your mindset around time.

The days and weeks fly by. You will die someday. Your body will start to fail you. Your kids will grow up and leave the house. Your parents will age and pass away. If you aren't deliberate and thoughtful, ten years will go by in a flash and you'll still be working the same dead-end job with the same unmotivated people. Your window and your ability to take risks will pass you by. It'll be too late.

I have an extreme scarcity mindset when it comes to time and I am very thoughtful about how I invest it. I've realized that it is the only thing that I'll never get back. If I spend $250,000 on a new business venture and it fails, it stings. But it is relative. You can always make more money. There is an infinite amount of money in this world, and it has your name on it if you spend your time making the right decisions and doing the right things.

But time is not this way. You have only so much. Be thoughtful.

Work on the Right Things

Most entrepreneurs don't end up owning a company.

They end up owning a job.

They run around servicing customers, putting out fires, solving problems, and trading their time for money *forever*. It's not because they're not smart enough. It's not because they don't work hard enough. And it's usually not even because they start the wrong business.

They simply do not work on the right things.

They focus on what's urgent and right in front of them instead of taking action on work that is important for the long-term growth of the company. They don't do the intellectually hard things. They don't have difficult conversations. They don't get uncomfortable and make moves on sales and hiring and delegation. They make the same mistakes and decisions over and over again but expect different results. They aren't good communicators or salespeople. They don't address fundamental problems when they arise and assume that they will just work out over time.

We all know this business owner. I have a friend from college who *is* this business owner.

He runs a pizza restaurant in Florida. It is on the best corner and is a beloved staple of the community. And they crush it. He takes home $250,000 per year from this fifteen-hundred-square-foot restaurant. He is building a great life for his family. He has taken the proceeds and bought some real estate and made other great investments. He lives in a nice house, and his kids go to private school even though he grew up an immigrant and his parents came here with nothing.

But here's the sad part:

He gets called to the restaurant every Thursday, Friday, and Saturday night by his management team to make pizzas when they get busy. He is stressed to the max. Every time I see him, I ask him about business, and he complains. About people. Customers. Equipment. Management.

My people suck. I can't find any good help. I can't afford a good manager. My customers are entitled and obnoxious. This is a hard business.

But why?

Many pizza restaurants are owned by people who aren't in the store flipping pizzas when things get busy. In most cases, a manager who makes $80,000 a year or less can run a pizza business and oversee the staff with little intervention or help from the owners. And many owners have figured out how to avoid owning a job so that they can own a business that makes them money while they do other things.

Don't get me wrong, the restaurant business is not easy. But I've seen many brands scale up to more than twenty restaurants and staff all of them. So I don't buy it.

My friend is stressed to the max and flipping pizzas every weekend because he works on the **urgent and important things** and not the **important things that aren't urgent**.

So let me introduce you to the four quadrants of time management.

There are four types of activities with different levels of importance and urgency.

The left side of the quadrant is urgent. These things must be done by somebody **now**. On the right side are the nonurgent things.

Here is the matrix using my friend's pizza business as an example:

#1 Important & Urgent	#2 Important & Not Urgent
Angry employee	Recruiting/Hiring/Training
Broken pizza oven	Sales/Business Development
Customer complaint	New technology adoption
Out of supplies	Planning and implementation
Comfortable and Hard	**Uncomfortable and Hard**
#3 Not Important & Urgent	#4 Not Important & Not Urgent
Customer phone call	Checking email constantly
Making a pizza	Busywork
Preparing supplies	Idle conversation
Cleaning kitchen	Sitting in traffic
Comfortable and Easy	**Comfortable and Easy**

Important and urgent things cannot wait. An employee calls with an issue. Your equipment malfunctions and business comes to a screeching halt. A customer is upset and calls or emails you. You run out of supplies and you can't fulfill orders.

These are fires, and as a business owner it's up to you to put them out right away or your business will suffer. However, everyone deals with this kind of thing—it's normal. Problem solving is a huge part of being successful, and these issues aren't necessarily scary or uncomfortable even if they are hard to deal with.

Not important and urgent tasks can still be critical to the business, but they're easily delegated as your business grows. Every business owner needs to do these things, especially in the beginning, but as the years go by and you hire the right people and put the right systems in place, you can and *should* spend less and less time here. The people you hire will be doing these things.

But my friend who runs the pizza shop spends almost all of his time in quadrant 3. All urgent stuff that is not important. He finds himself stuck doing the work to run the business. He makes pizzas when he is shorthanded. He is answering the phone when nobody is at the register. He runs to the store to get supplies if he runs out.

Here is the thing about quadrant 3:

It feels very productive. It is the default thing to do. Go to work and do the job. Flip the pizzas. Answer the phone when it rings. Delegating is hard and getting somebody else in place to own the work isn't easy, so a lot of business owners default to staying right here.

Get out of my way, I'll handle it. The buck stops with me.

Not important and not urgent tasks are time wasters. Repeatedly checking emails or social media. Small talk or sitting in traffic. Busywork around the office that doesn't move the needle. This stuff should be removed from your schedule. All those tasks may make you feel important, but they are crutches and time wasters. And most people use them to avoid doing hard things.

Cold hard truth:
Doing the important but not urgent tasks is the key to your business growth.

Almost every single good thing that has ever happened in my business has come as a result of spending time in the **important and not urgent** quadrant. Starting my first business wasn't urgent. I could have just as easily sat back and continued to drink beer with my college buddies that week in Ithaca, New York.

Instead, in 2011, I started working on something that had the potential to pay me back a few weeks later, a few years later, and then nine years later with a seven-figure exit. I did it because I wanted to build something and got excited by the concept of entrepreneurship and making money.

Then, in 2016, we started building that first self-storage facility with a plan of making money several years down the road. It wasn't urgent. I could easily have just kept driving trucks and answering phones at my moving and storage company.

Four years ago I recruited and hired a key employee who took over my job at my real estate company. That freed up a lot of time so I could focus on big decisions rather than dealing with bankers and investors and underwriting every deal. I didn't have to make that hire. It wasn't urgent, but it was important. Since then I've been able to focus on other important but not urgent things like marketing strategy, promotions to get customers in the door, hiring an acquisition team to find more deals, training and hiring a sales team to rent more units, and even pursuing other ventures like acquiring Somewhere.com.

Successful people and great business owners spend *a lot* of their time in the important but not urgent quadrant. They focus on marketing *before* they need more business. They focus on attracting talent *before* their organization is overloaded with work. When they get too busy to spend time in this quadrant, they hire and delegate so they can go back to working on these high-leverage activities.

My friend who runs the pizza business could definitely do the hard and uncomfortable work to recruit and hire an operations manager for $80,000 a year. He'd be able to spend his time making the business more efficient and would likely be able to increase profitability or maybe just make $170,000 a year instead of $250,000. But he'd have his time back. He'd very likely be able to earn even more money elsewhere doing higher-leverage activities than flipping pizzas on Saturdays.

When you work in quadrant 2, you are delaying gratification. You are doing work today that will give you a reward four weeks or two months or even five years down the road.

Hiring and training employees is the best example of an important but not urgent activity. It is always uncomfortable. You can almost always get by without them for a few more days or do the job yourself. But it allows you to gain back your time and work on more important things.

Sales is also an extremely high-leverage activity in the important but not urgent category. Going out and chasing more business is uncomfortable and easy to put off for another day. But it is the key to growth.

Demoing and implementing new technology can drastically improve the efficiency of your business, but you could get by with your handwritten notes just a bit longer for sure.

The media will tell you that entrepreneurship is just a giant stress fest. Running around putting out fires. Solving urgent problems. Rushing from customer to customer and staying up 24/7 to meet deadlines.

It doesn't have to be that way.

Great entrepreneurs are able to take a step back and figure out where their energy could yield the most long-term results for the company.

The 80/20 Rule

An unfortunate truth:

No matter how efficient you are, most of the stuff you work on will not move the needle.

There is a power law when it comes to your business and your results. You've heard of the Pareto principle before because it's true:

Twenty percent of your activities will generate 80 percent of your positive outcomes and growth.

The other 80 percent of your time will be spent doing things that don't move things forward very much. It's a small subset of very high-leverage activities that generate outsize results.

I once did some consulting for a podcast listener who ran a poop-scooping business. It was a great company with six full-time employees, six trucks, and about $200,000 in annual take-home profit just for him. He asked me what I thought about growing his business, and the first thing I did was go on the company's website and try to sign up for his services.

The whole process was clunky. The website form didn't make sense. It was tucked below some text that wasn't clear. I could tell he was losing a lot of potential customers on this page. I would have navigated away in a heartbeat had I been an actual customer. You never get a second chance to make a first impression, and this first impression was terrible.

So we fixed it. He spent about thirty hours one week revamping this flow. He put some clear text at the top of the page on how his service worked. He added a simple form with a "get a quote" button. The process was much clearer. By collecting the email addresses of potential customers, he was able to contact them and make the sale.

His new customer leads doubled overnight, and the company

ended up doubling in size over the next twenty-four months. That one little decision made a big difference and was part of the 20 percent of effort that resulted in 80 percent of his growth.

This power law doesn't just apply when it comes to your own work. It applies to everyone who is a part of your business. That includes vendors, employees, and customers. One thing I've found to be true in any business is that 20 percent of your customers will generate 80 percent of your headache, and 20 percent of your customers will generate 80 percent of your profit. The sooner you realize these aren't the same customers, the sooner you can build a great business.

If you want to go even further, you can apply the 80/20 principle to virtually every area of your life and business. Twenty percent of your exercise leads to 80 percent of your fitness gains. Twenty percent of your relationships lead to 80 percent of your joy and happiness. And 20 percent of your effort and business decisions will drive 80 percent of your profit and results.

So which activities fall into the 20 percent of high-leverage activities?

It's the same activities that are defined as "important and not urgent" in the four quadrants of time management.

These high-leverage activities fall into quadrant 2 of the matrix. Sales. Hiring. Delegation. Training. Decision making. New opportunity exploration. Meetings with potential partners and employees. Networking. Competition research. And more.

You can (and should) analyze your schedule based on the four quadrants and this 20 percent rule.

My ask of you right now:

1. Go through your schedule and write down exactly what activities you are doing. Log the time you dedicate to each one for a given week.

2. Next to every activity on your list, write down a yes or a no if you think it is potentially a 20 percent activity that would generate 80 percent of your progress.
3. Next to each activity also write the quadrant. Is it important and urgent? Is it urgent but not that important? Is it not important and not urgent? Could an activity be completely deleted from your life?
4. Now adjust your schedule to focus on the 20 percent and do more of the important stuff that isn't urgent!

I do this practice at least once a year. I log my time for a week, and then I get up before my kids one morning, think on my activities, and categorize them based on importance, urgency, and likelihood of being in the 20 percent high-leverage zone. I adjust as needed.

If you put your head in the sand and work eighty hours a week without stepping back to do a bit of planning and asset allocation (yes, your time is an asset), you're making a mistake. When you are in the weeds of your business, it is easy to overlook what is important. It is easy to ignore and put off the hard decisions you need to make or the hard conversations you need to have.

Hold yourself accountable and do this analysis. It works.

What gets measured is more likely to improve. Make time for this—it's part of the important, nonurgent work, too.

Do Things Today That Will Reward You Seventy Years Down the Road

Entrepreneurship is like an adult marshmallow test.

Most people aren't wealthy and successful because they're unwilling to trade short-term loss for long-term gain. They make decisions that maximize pleasure today, tomorrow, or next week instead of looking to the future and making decisions that will maximize results five to ten years down the road.

Unfortunately, most people think of entrepreneurship as a get-rich-quick scheme. The media likes to celebrate stories of people who went from their college dorm rooms to being billionaires in just a few years. But these unicorns are one-in-a-million success stories. And the truth is that entrepreneurship is anything but a get-rich-quick scheme.

A close friend of mine is a real estate investor and developer in Nashville. Makes seven figures a year. Owns and controls more than $100 million of apartment buildings in the best neighborhoods in the city. How long did it take him to get wealthy?

His story goes back three generations to the first members of his family who came to New York City. His great-grandparents were the first ones over, and they worked hourly jobs their whole lives, so their children and grandchildren could go to college.

Then his parents became doctors so they could create an even better life for their kids and give them more opportunity. By the time my friend was fifteen, his parents owned a few apartment buildings they had bought with the extra income from their earnings, and my friend began to learn a little bit about real estate.

He went to a great private school in Nashville. Then to Duke. He met folks there who had serious capital. He took their investment and bought his first apartment building when he was thirty. Then, he built his firm over the next twelve years to get to where he is today.

What people don't realize:

It took my friend's family seventy years of work to get to the upper rungs of society. His grandparents were immigrants. They worked for forty years just to send their kids, his parents, to a decent college. His parents then worked for another thirty years to send him to a private high school and give him the opportunity to go to the Ivy League.

This was a seventy-year, multigenerational game.

And you want it all right now?

For almost everyone, generational wealth in America is a *very* long game. So long that it takes multiple generations! People immigrate to America with nothing. They work hard just to get by, feed their families, and set their kids up with more opportunity than they had. Those kids get professional or blue-collar jobs and climb a rung on the ladder of society. They become doctors or lawyers or plumbers or welders and create stability and a backstop for their kids. And then those kids use that backstop and safety net to become entrepreneurs and accumulate even more wealth.

The lesson:

Play the long game.

Understand that building wealth is a process. You must suffer and do hard and boring things for many years to have great results. While everyone else is making decisions to maximize their enjoyment right now, successful people make decisions to maximize their enjoyment years from now. Being in the trenches improving day in and day out for years is what sets you up to capitalize on the larger, more enticing, more profitable opportunities.

That is the funny thing about entrepreneurship.

You can toil away for weeks or months or years and feel as if you are making no progress at all. Then, in a matter of weeks, it can all come together, you gain traction, and you make massive strides.

If you're doing it right and setting yourself up to capitalize on opportunities, the growth can come at you fast and when you least expect it.

Sprints happen, that is for sure. Opportunities arise and you have to spend weeks or months flat out, seizing the opportunity. But then it goes back to the monotonous grind. Doing the right things over and over again for years on end and living with the less than comfortable feelings that brings.

Think of it this way:

Entrepreneurship is a lot like hunting.

The entrepreneur is a lion out in the Sahara lying on a rock, toiling away in his business doing the boring, not fun stuff. Then, all of a sudden, a gazelle appears in the field. That gazelle is an opportunity worth sprinting after.

The lion gets up and sprints full speed. One hundred percent energy for a few moments. The entrepreneur seizes the opportunity and carries it back to his company, and it keeps everyone full and fed for a long time. Then he goes back to sitting on the rock. Your job as the leader of the company is to chase down the opportunity, kill it, and bring it back for everyone to eat.

But those days are few and far between. The rest of the time you're lying on a rock. Sitting back watching your team work and making sure everybody has everything they need to do their job. Grinding away. If you can't survive the boring stuff, your company won't be around to take part in the hunting.

Chapter 8

Get Your Shit Together

Remember the sidewalk chalk and flyers we used for marketing in the early days?

It worked really well—*almost too well.*

By the end of the 2013 spring season in Boston, we had more than seven hundred customers and a full 7,000-square-foot warehouse at 167 Bow Street in Everett, Massachusetts.

Over five thousand individual boxes, suitcases, bins, and other random things.

Unfortunately, we picked up all that stuff with inexperienced employees, terrible processes, and little to no sleep. I can say for sure we *did not* do a good job organizing the warehouse or labeling items.

The entire city of Boston moves back to school on Labor Day weekend. By August 20th, I knew we were in trouble.

I spent fifteen hours a day that week moving things around. Trying to complete orders and get ready. Before we had returned a single box, I was already physically sore from the manual labor. On top of that, I fell behind on scheduling deliveries and employees. So I had to fit that task in from 4:00 a.m. to 8:00 a.m. before I began loading trucks.

The mayhem really started after I sent out the initial schedule to all seven hundred customers a few days before the first delivery. Almost immediately, I had more than two hundred change requests and other customer service inquiries. But unfortunately, that wasn't my biggest problem. To make the deliveries work, I needed ten full-time employees on September 1, 2, and 3. When the morning of the first came, I had just eight.

Three employees stayed back at the warehouse pulling orders and preparing for the next day. The rest of us spread out across five trucks with my partner, his brother, and me each running a truck all by ourselves.

If anyone was going down with the ship, it was going to be me.

From 8:00 a.m. to 2:00 p.m., I drove the box truck, answered customer service calls, and hand-delivered boxes to the Bay State Road brownstones on BU's campus. Every single box had to go up at least two flights of stairs. Sometimes three or four. I didn't have time to eat or rest, plus I had nearly killed myself the past week in the warehouse.

In addition to being exhausted, I was chafing horribly and bleeding at the tops of my thighs. I got back to the warehouse at 3:00 p.m., picked up another full truck, and set out alone to deliver it all. I managed to get that truck emptied by 10:00 p.m. I had a fever of 102 and my jeans were stained with blood. I threw away the clothes, took ibuprofen, and spent the night answering customer service calls, making schedules, and loading trucks for the next day.

By then, I had gone three days without sleep. I don't remember much of day two, but I do remember wondering what the hell I was doing with my life. If I had doubted my path senior year, this was a million times worse. I put my feelings aside. Then Dan and I spent all night loading up the five trucks for the next day's morning shift.

Morning came, our third consecutive day of loading and unloading trucks and the biggest number of deliveries yet. My team was taking a beating. They were exhausted from working forty hours in three days, and their tips sucked because I had done a poor job with the schedule. Several of them didn't show, but I remember the kids who stuck with us by name. I would kill for those kids now. They laid it all on the line—never complaining—and not surprisingly, they've all moved on to bigger and better things and are ultra successful all these years later.

On the afternoon of the third day, the phone rang as I stood on Park Drive near the intersection of Buswell Street on Boston University's South Campus. I had just delivered ten items up five flights to the top of a brownstone, and my truck was empty. I glanced at the number. I knew from experience that when a call came in from my partner or an employee during our most chaotic times, it was never good news.

"Nick, I'm so sorry," one of my employees said when I answered, "but I hit a parked BMW at Harvard with the box truck." *Ding*—he texted me a photo. He hadn't just tapped it. He had destroyed the entire side of the car including the rear quarter panel, both doors, and the front quarter panel. The BMW was probably totaled.

We'd already had our fair share of accidents during the previous few days. One employee put gasoline in a diesel engine, which left us with a repair bill of more than $5,000 not covered by insurance. Another employee hit an overhang at HoJo dorm—also on Boston University's campus—and ripped the top off one of our trucks. Also not covered by insurance.

Now this.

If the employee had done it in a rental, it would have been fine because we had insurance on all of them. But this was our truck, and the claim was on my personal insurance policy because we hadn't been able to get business coverage.

I put my head down for a second. I was trying to figure out what to do. That's when my partner dialed in. One of our other employees had just quit and left a full truck on Northeastern's campus. He was fed up with the long hours, so he locked the truck, hid the key, and texted Dan to say he was done (and thankfully to tell him where the key was hidden).

The problem? That truck still had boxes for twenty-five customers. We were already two hours late on that schedule, which should have started at 1:00 p.m. My truck was empty, but I was supposed to go back to the warehouse and get my second truck of the day. Instead, I needed to go to Northeastern.

I had been ignoring customer calls all day as I delivered box after box, but now the calls were coming in hot, one per minute. I sat down on the curb and hit ignore. Another call. I hit ignore again. Then another.

It was right about then that I slipped into a full-on anxiety attack. It crept in over thirty seconds and then flooded me all at once. My chest tightened up. I was hysterical. I began to weep. I curled up in a little ball on the side of the road. I felt out of control. In over my head. As far as I was concerned, my business—and my future—were slipping away right in front of me. It was all my fault.

I picked up the phone and called my mom.

All I wanted was to be back at home in Indiana instead of in this big city going through hell and losing money. My right foot had locked up from the constant gas/brake transition while driving the truck. I hadn't slept in nearly a week. I was bleeding between my legs.

My hands were blistered and cracked. And I had lost twenty pounds off my six-foot, three-inch frame.

She tried to console me, but she couldn't.

Next, I called my partner. "I can't do this. It's over," I said, crying into the phone.

"Get your shit together," he said. "I'm in hell, too, but if you lay down on me, we're screwed. Remember how we said we were in this together? If anybody can do this, you can."

He lifted me up and pulled me out of my anxiety-fueled spiral.

I hung up and spent the next fifteen minutes getting myself together. I got in the truck. I drove to the other truck. I kept ignoring the calls and kept delivering boxes.

Twenty-four hours later it was all over.

The phone stopped ringing. The warehouse was nearly empty. We slept and ate.

And I came out the other side a harder man with a new perspective on what being an entrepreneur really means. I'm thankful for that experience to this day, but this life isn't for everyone.

Every business or project or hobby is fun in the beginning because the progress is coming fast and furious. You're improving by leaps and bounds. You're getting the first customers. You're launching a website and designing a logo. It is full speed and exciting. Then comes the realization that it's grueling work to build a business. Business is hard. Life is hard. It is difficult to achieve success. If it were easy, the world would be full of fit, happy, rich business owners.

Stress, fear, and discomfort are unfortunate parts of business and life.

If you're doing anything worth doing, you will encounter situations that lead to fear, anxiety, and a number of other unpleasant emotions. Unfortunately, the world doesn't care about you and your feelings. Bad things happen to great people and great operators. We are gamblers after all, and doing business requires a level of comfort with the risk of things going wrong.

> **Cold hard truth:**
> There is a direct correlation between the stress you have endured in your professional life and the amount of money you earn today.

Stress is natural. It's normal. Discomfort is a good thing. It makes you stronger and better. The only way is to push through it and accept it as part of what it takes to be successful.

I am and have always been the type of person who thrives under pressure. I feel best when I am growing, improving, and pushing myself. My advice to you is to embrace the challenge and learn to thrive under pressure.

Lose the Victim Mentality

The media, especially social media, will lead you to believe that the world is worse than it has ever been.

People are suffering more than ever. Our lives are more dangerous than ever. The world is more unfair than ever.

Look at the headlines. Flip on the news.

You'll undoubtedly read about how our food is poisoning us. Entire groups of people are being mistreated and have zero opportunity. We have an energy crisis. Pollution is destroying our planet. Our neighborhoods are dangerous. Our kids are at risk of death or mistreatment around every corner. Our schools are terrible and unsafe. The employment market is tough. The average worker is mistreated and overworked. Business is brutally hard, and success just isn't possible.

Let me tell you right now:

None of that is true.

Life is better and easier than ever before. Poor people today have a better life than wealthy people fifty years ago. Crime is at an all-time low. Kids are safer now than at any point in history. The internet has created more opportunities for more people than ever before. Workplaces are safer and cleaner, and workers have more options and mobility than at any time in history.

This is objectively true. There is no disputing it. The data supports it.

So what gives?

Fear sells. Doomsday articles get clicks. They get shared. People relish and find comfort in drama and pain.

And it has spawned a huge portion of the population who feel like victims. It isn't their fault they aren't happy, healthy, or successful at what they are trying to do, they tell themselves. It is hard out there! The world is a bad place. We have terrible disadvantages, and there is so much wrong with the world. It's all holding us back! Our careers are an uphill battle, and entrepreneurship is impossible.

Cold hard truth:

You are not a victim. Your situation right now is a direct result of your decisions and your actions in the past. Your relationships, your income, your physical and mental health, your assets, your network. **The buck stops with you.**

This might hurt. This is likely hard to swallow:

It isn't anyone else's fault. Your life today is a direct result of your own decisions and actions.

Successful people understand this and take ownership in *every* situation. If you cultivate resilience, you have a significant competitive advantage over most people. If you are willing to do hard things, your tolerance for discomfort will become a superpower. If you swim against the current and try something new that might lead to a different result from the majority of people, you learn to adapt to difficult conditions without constantly looking for someone or something to blame.

You, and only you, are responsible for your life, your business, and your future.

Not a politician. Not your parents. Not the economy. Not the world around you. *You.* If you can accept that fact, embrace it even, no one person or situation can shake you.

Get Good at Having Uncomfortable Conversations

In 2015, Dan and I decided to build a self-storage facility from the ground up. Looking back, it was stupid. We should have just bought an operational facility and made it better, but we were young and arrogant and simply didn't think about doing it the easy way.

Even though Storage Squad was going well, we realized it wasn't sustainable. The market wasn't large enough, the stress was too high, and the revenue potential wasn't there to build a large, scalable business. That said, we were learning a shit ton about operations, management, and delegation, which would prove to be invaluable over time.

Unfortunately, there was one lesson we hadn't learned yet.

Based on our initial analysis, I calculated that we would need $1.9 million for construction. So I built a 120-page package with our underwriting, marketing plan, and budget and set up meetings. The first ten banks turned me down.

The eleventh, Tompkins Trust Company, said yes and agreed to lend us $1.5 million.

Then I sat down with more than a hundred potential investors. Ninety-five of them turned me down, but five said yes. One was my dad and one was Steve, the real estate agent who had sold us the $250,000 parcel of land. Let's face it—I was selling whoever I could.

We broke ground in June 2016, a few days before my wedding. Steve's check cleared just before we had to make a $100,000 payment to our earthwork contractor. It came just in the nick of time.

Construction continued into 2017, and by January we realized we had a big problem. We were way over budget. Like more than 25 percent over budget to the tune of $500,000. We were racing to open in time for the student rush in 2017, and we did all of our concrete pouring in the dead of winter. We had to heat the slabs with pipes and water heaters for three weeks after pouring. It was a disaster.

Then steel prices jumped to record highs before we ordered our building—our delay there was a $50,000 mistake alone. Problem after problem came up. At every turn, I was sure we could get back on track. Sure that I didn't need to let anyone know *just yet* about our budget and construction issues.

But finally, our costs were so high I had no choice. I went back with my tail between my legs to Tompkins Trust and all five of my investors asking for 25 percent more money. I remember that conference call as if it were yesterday. Monday, January 16, 2017. I couldn't sleep all weekend.

They were visibly upset about the news. One of the investors grilled me with several pointed rhetorical questions. I couldn't do anything but take ownership, apologize, and tell them the project would succeed if we just got it done.

In the end, we got our certificate of occupancy with a building that was half finished and didn't have a roof on one side. Students started moving in immediately. We had no fence, gravel drives, no HVAC, and half of our upper level was still under construction when we started renting units.

By the time we were officially finished with the development, we had spent $2.4 million.

And I felt like a broken man.

I'm happy to report that five years later my partner and I bought out our investors at an $8 million valuation and we now own 100 percent of the building.

My father hadn't told me that to make his initial $125,000 investment in the project, he had taken out a mortgage on my childhood home. Looking back, I'm happy I didn't know. It would have amplified my stress and anxiety.

We bought him out in 2022 for $520,000, and that is now a massive chunk of his net worth.

> **Cold hard truth:**
> One difficult conversation at the beginning of an endeavor or relationship will save you ten hard conversations later.
> It will also save you a lot of stress.

Too many people are afraid to tell others what they don't want to hear. Instead of having hard conversations at the beginning, they'll put themselves up against impossible deadlines.

And they'll be in hell just as we were when they can't deliver.

A lot of customers are needy, demanding, and straight up unrealistic. They will manipulate you to make promises so that they can get what they want. But lots of business owners shoot themselves in the foot by agreeing to those demands or pretending things are going well when they aren't.

There's plenty of blame to go around.

You have to have the courage to stand up for yourself and keep this from happening. You have to be brave enough to take responsibility early and often. There is no other way.

Practice Fear Setting

Every time I feel overwhelmed or I'm about to take a chance on something, I do a simple exercise. I sit down in front of a blank page or document on my computer and write out the absolute worst-case scenario.

You can do this, too.

Question 1: If the worst possible outcome happens, what does it look like?

Go ahead and write down the answer. Be dramatic. Think of your absolute nightmare and spell it out in detail.

The worst-case scenario for me is always bankruptcy. Running out of money and having to start over. I've written it down a few times.

Question 2: What is the worst result of this scenario? What happens next?

Follow the worst-case scenario to its logical conclusion.

My answers?

I have skills. I live in America where bankruptcy isn't permanent.

I have a family that loves me and a wife who supports me. I have parents with two spare bedrooms I could move into, and my kids wouldn't know the difference. I wouldn't go hungry. Neither would my family. I'd be able to get a W-2 job for more than $200,000 per year almost instantly. I'd be able to bootstrap a business or get partners and grow a new company. I'd come out stronger, hungrier, and more motivated than ever.

I didn't do this exercise in Boston when I had my anxiety attack on the side of the road. But if I had, it would have looked something like this:

The worst-case scenario:

I have a lot of unhappy customers who are going to ask for refunds. It will be expensive, probably around $100,000. I will deliver items two or three days late to customers who will have to go without sheets and bedding in their new dorm rooms for the first few nights. I'll get yelled at. I'll get a bunch of Yelp reviews and Google reviews trashing my company.

What is the *worst* result of this? If things go as horribly as possible, what *could* happen?

We could go this year without making any money. We might even lose money. The business would be in poor shape, and we might even have to shut it down. I would have to go and find a better business with fewer logistics and less stress. Or I could just get a job and build a successful career the old-fashioned way.

I'd still be me. I'm not bankrupt. I'm not unemployable. I'm not in jail. My wife wouldn't leave me.

My family still has those two empty bedrooms back in the house I grew up in.

No matter how many times I tell myself that I'll be okay no matter what, the fear is real. It probably will be for you, too. Our identities are wrapped up in our businesses and our careers. People measure us based on how much money we make, how many employees we have, and how successful financially we are. So when we fail, or even consider the possibility of failure, the pain can be unbearable. We can't stand to think about how shameful and embarrassing it would be to tell our families and friends or have people find out that we lost it all.

Luckily, most situations aren't this dire. Not even close. I've done fear setting many times where the results were laughable. Case in point, I was super stressed about going into a meeting where I knew I had to have a very difficult conversation with a great friend who was also an employee. He wasn't pulling his weight, and I knew the conversation might end with us severing our professional relationship.

The absolute worst-case scenario? I say something I can't take back, and it ruins our friendship. But I knew that wouldn't happen. I could control this. *Don't get emotional*, I told myself. *Think before you talk.*

The more likely worst case? We split up, and it is hurtful. But then I help him find a new job, and he goes on to crush it somewhere else.

All I had to do was look at the words on the paper and take a deep breath. The stress went away. I was prepared and ready to attack the situation, knowing that the worst-case scenario was manageable and not that bad.

You can use this strategy in all areas of life.

What is the worst thing that can happen when you approach a beautiful person at a bar? What is the worst thing that can happen when you cold-call somebody to get them to buy something from you? What is the worst thing that can happen if you try to get that employee to join your company and they decline the offer?

Rejection? Them hanging up on you? Big deal. You walk away two seconds later in the same situation as you are in today.

How is that scary? Why is it scary?

This exercise helps you put it all in perspective so you can improve your ability to deal with stress. Because the more stress you can handle, the more money you will make. And the more comfortable you can get in uncomfortable situations, the more effective you will be at everything in life.

Be Resourceful

At the end of the day, there are no answers in entrepreneurship. There are only options.

Every decision has about ten potential paths you can choose. Each one will be combined with several other decisions and could yield a wide array of potential outcomes, many of which are totally out of your control. Luck is a big part of it. Decision making matters, too.

But ultimately, it all comes down to resourcefulness.

In high school they try to make us think that life will be like a textbook. That if you need to find the answer, you just flip a few pages back and look it up. That there is a right or wrong answer to every potential decision and that every problem can be studied and figured out with structure, memorization, or logic.

That couldn't be further from the truth.

Business, like the world, is emotional and dynamic. Most problems are people problems, and people aren't simple or logical. They are emotional and their needs and demands change often. For every business problem, there are ten ways you can approach it. There are ten or even a hundred factors influencing the results or inputs.

If you are looking for answers, you're not going to find them. It's all on you. You, and you alone, are tasked with weighing the factors and making gut decisions on how to approach things. Luck can present you with opportunities, but if you don't know how to make decisions, you'll quickly fail and squander your potential.

People don't understand just how many decisions need to be made until they're tasked with running a growing company. Who are we going to hire? How much are we going to pay them? Where are we going to find them? How are we going to market? How much are we going to spend on it? What are we going to charge? How are we going to solve these twenty problems a day?

It is nonstop. Decision making is a skill. The only way to get better is to practice.

Practice making these decisions. For better or worse, you'll get instant feedback. If you come in with an open mind, you'll be able to adapt and overcome the bad decisions. Nobody gets every decision right. You can make half of your decisions incorrectly and still win if you get the big stuff right. Just put yourself out there and practice.

Part III
People

Chapter 9

The Attributes of Winners

Once upon a time, I was the bottleneck of every important part of my real estate company.

We had eight full-time employees and six properties, but I was the one who made every decision. I took every investor meeting. I replied to every email from every banker regarding the numerous loans we had on our properties.

I wrote the investor updates each month. I handled the negotiations when we were looking to acquire a property. I did the underwriting and made the final call on every purchase after analyzing the numbers with a fine-tooth comb.

These were high-value, high-stakes decisions.

What properties were we going to buy and how much were we going to pay? How would we raise the capital? What terms could we get from banks and how could we get them confident enough to lend us the money?

I had no plans to delegate this stuff. Way too important.

Fast-forward to July 2022 when something I never thought could happen ended up happening.

We closed on a $9 million deal in Abingdon, Virginia, and I had absolutely no part in it.

I didn't find the deal. I didn't underwrite the deal. I didn't meet with any investors. I didn't visit the property. I didn't talk to a single banker.

All I did was look at and approve the offer my team sent and then sign the Docusign package on closing day.

My team ran the due diligence. They negotiated with the seller and quarterbacked the deal to closing and contract signature. They raised nearly $5 million of capital from twenty-four investors. They took all the meetings. They secured the bank loan for $4.5 million.

Then we owned the building and our team was on-site during the first week. They changed the signage. They installed a security system. They put all of the customers into our software and welcomed them to our company.

It all just happened. Without me.

How?

People.

Good people in the right seats with the right processes who were able to do tasks and make decisions on behalf of me and the company.

Recruiting, hiring, and delegation are the keys to success in the world of entrepreneurship.

The Ultimate Form of Leverage

As an entrepreneur, I've spent nearly all of my energy for fifteen years persuading other people to join me on this journey. To work for one of my companies, trust me, buy from me, invest with me, or partner with me.

When it comes to entrepreneurship, people are the ultimate form of leverage.

I've had a lot of success:

My companies employ more than 300 people. My companies do over $30 million a year in revenue. I've raised money from more than 250 individuals. I have more than 15 people who have ownership stakes and operational roles in my businesses. I've interviewed thousands. I've personally convinced more than 30 people in management roles to leave their jobs to come work with me.

I've also made many mistakes.

I've navigated uncomfortable conversations with employees or customers who were upset for one reason or another. I've delivered criticism and bad news more times than I can count.

I had to fire one of my best friends who stood up in my wedding a few months earlier. I've had an employee cry in my arms because they didn't know what they were doing with their life, and I couldn't create the opportunity for them that I thought I could.

I've had brutally hard negotiations with partners I was trying to buy out of my companies because they weren't pulling their weight. I've fired family members. I've renegotiated deals I believed weren't win-win situations, and I've had partners come to me to renegotiate deals I *thought* were win-win situations.

The one thing I'm very proud of?

You won't find anybody who walked away from an interaction with me feeling as if I screwed them over. That guy who stood up in my wedding and got let go from my company is still a great friend to this day.

Another thing I'm proud of is that, generally, good people do not leave my companies. I've been able to retain key employees for years and years at many of my businesses.

I attract great people who are insanely productive because I do the work to set them up for success. I properly manage expectations. I do what I say I'm going to do. I'm always honest with them even if it hurts. I'm respectful and have their best interests at heart. I'm not greedy, and I'm happy to pay my people exceptionally well if they add value to my businesses.

But dealing with people is hard.

People are not predictable. They will constantly surprise you in pleasant and unpleasant ways. Relationships aren't rational. They are emotional.

I talk to a lot of people who work normal jobs following directions at a normal company but are considering entrepreneurship.

My first question is always the same:

Do you like dealing with other people? Can you manage egos and emotions and desires and the roller coaster of depending on other humans to work with you and around you and for you?

The answer is very often no.

But dealing with people is something you have to do all day, every day as an entrepreneur. And like sales, it doesn't come naturally to anybody. You must accept the discomfort. You must call yourself an extrovert (even if you aren't) and become one. You must practice and put in the reps and build the muscle.

I have a lot to learn and I am not perfect. I will continue to make mistakes. I am a work in progress, and I am by no means the best in the world at communication or relationships or management. But on the following pages I'll do my very best to tell you everything I know about dealing with people, bringing them into your organization, creating win-win situations, and turning these people into assets.

If you can unlock and master the art of dealing with people, you will have the ability to build companies, and you will become wealthy.

It's as simple as that. There will be nothing that holds you back, and the world will be at your fingertips.

Who Do We Want on Our Team?

Your company is only as strong as the people you hire.

The right people will climb with you to the top, but they'll also stand by you, come up with solutions, and work hard to get themselves and everyone else out of the hole when it's not smooth sailing.

Life throws curveballs.

Business is hard and stressful. There is nothing worse than being surrounded by the wrong people when the going gets tough.

> **Cold hard truth:**
> Most entrepreneurs are far too passive when it comes to relationships and investments in people.

They settle for whoever is nearby without analyzing what values these people have, how they think, where they are headed, and what that means for them personally and for the future of their companies.

We're also far too slow to remove people from our lives and organizations.

"We should forgive people. We should work to improve people. We should give them second chances and cut them some slack."

I totally disagree with this.

The good thing about bad and incompetent people is that they show you who they are fairly quickly. People who rob and steal will continue to rob and steal. People with emotional disorders will show radical behavior fairly quickly. People who manipulate others will fall back on this behavior to get their way fairly quickly. Incompetent employees will make boneheaded decisions on day one.

As the saying goes:

When people show you who they are, believe them.

But on the flip side, there is nothing more rewarding than being surrounded by great people doing great things. Driven people. Hardworking people. People who make good decisions and have your best interests in mind.

Walking into a business meeting with a master negotiator on your team is a great feeling. I've been there.

Marrying a woman who has her shit together and makes great decisions for your family is a weapon and an asset. I know because I found one.

So who do we want on our team? Who do we want in our corner? It comes down to five kinds of people who add the most to our businesses and our lives. Let's explain each type.

People with an Abundance Mindset

Have you ever watched crabs in a bucket? Just when one of them is about to escape, the others grab hold and pull it back down. The crabs do not want to see the other crabs make it out. By their very nature, they keep each other from winning.

Unfortunately, a huge portion of the population is just like these crabs. They go through life with a negative mindset. Every day is a zero-sum game. In order for them to win, somebody else needs to lose. In order for them to make money, somebody else has to miss out.

Too many people in the world today think that there is only so much money and success to be had and somebody else succeeding is holding them back. "If Nick makes a dollar, that is a dollar that I can't make myself! Therefore, I must hold Nick back and keep secrets from him."

That is total bullshit. Run away from people with this mindset.

People succeeding around you and getting rich makes it *more likely* that you will also succeed. If you make a dollar, it is not because you took a dollar from somebody else. It is because you added value in excess of the money that traded hands.

Surround yourself with people who share this mindset and who want to see you win.

We live in a world of abundance. There is a growing resource pile, and *everyone* can get some at the same time. Especially when it comes to entrepreneurship.

The most successful people all share this mindset. Others winning is good for me, too. So I'll celebrate success and cheer others on. I'll lift others up. I'll do my part so everyone can win.

People with a Sense of Urgency

Surround yourself with people who make things happen quickly. Who default to action. They shoot first and aim later. They are willing to move at an uncomfortable speed with a half-built system and a shaky, uncertain plan.

In business, especially before your company matures, you have to iterate quickly.

Experiment, learn, adjust, and experiment again. Especially in the first years of your company, this is a must-have trait. These people work faster, they are more efficient, they make things happen. Unfortunately, this is something you can't teach. Either someone makes things happen quickly and understands that business is a race or they don't.

Your management team in the early days should consist only of people like this. If you have people who need to get something done for the business but it takes them a week, you will suffer. Your only advantage as a small, new business is that you can move quickly. You are at a disadvantage against your competitors in every other way.

Build a team who can take advantage.

People Who Are Not Afraid to Stand Up to You and Call You Out

The worst thing you can do as a leader is surround yourself with people who agree with you no matter what and blindly follow your lead. Instead, you want to build a business full of smart people who think critically and look at things in a new way. And you want to encourage them to speak up and be supportive and open-minded when they do.

This is hard. This is uncomfortable. It can be infuriating when people call you out or disagree with you. It takes swallowing your ego and your pride and admitting when you are wrong.

But it is also invaluable.

I have one of these individuals on my team at my storage company, and he has saved my ass several times. We hired Kevin as the VP of Finance in 2020. 2021 was a busy year, and great deals were plentiful. We bought $50 million worth of storage.

Then in 2022, things began to shift. The deals weren't quite as good, and other buyers were bidding up prices to levels that weren't sustainable. But I was still optimistic. I was still confident in our strategy.

Kevin went on vacation for five days in early 2022, and while he was gone, I made offers on four properties. Two of the offers were accepted. These two deals amounted to about $10 million worth of storage.

When Kevin came back, he called a meeting.

"Nick, we can't pay this much for these buildings. These are not good deals. Too much risk. Too much debt. We need to drop these contracts."

He was right, but his assessment embarrassed me and hurt my ego. I've spent my entire career pushing and aggressively pursuing the next opportunity. At that time the market was heating up to unsustainable levels, and the deals were indeed risky. What if rates went up? After the meeting, I knew we needed to drop the contracts, so I took responsibility for the mistake and did the work of breaking the bad news to our team and to the sellers.

Kevin's willingness to call me out saved us.

The market weakened, debt got exponentially more expensive over the following twenty-four months, and these deals would have been very stressful to refinance and hold for the long run.

Kevin having the courage to call out the boss saved the ship, and our discipline and patience in 2022 and 2023 paid off.

People Who Make Good Decisions

If I look back on my career, there is one glaring pattern:

I overestimated the ability of many people.

I assumed competence and ability in almost everyone. Especially during the first years of my business, I hired very fast and put up with low performance from my employees for far too long.

This person can do the job for sure! It is simple!

I was wrong.

I've been let down time and time again by the decision-making ability of other people. And I've hung on too long trying to improve the decision-making ability of people who've already made poor decisions and caused stress in the company or cost the company money.

The good news is that not everyone in your company needs to make decisions. A lot of folks can follow directions, pay attention to detail, and add value. But when it comes to management and higher-skilled roles, you must find the good decision makers.

How do you know who is good and who isn't?

You watch them make decisions. You ask questions of them and hear their reasoning. And you watch the results of those decisions.

People Who Aren't Afraid to Get Their Hands Dirty and Do the Work

A lot of people want to delegate everything and be visionaries.

These are not the people you want in your corner in the early days. You must find people who are willing to swallow their pride and get sweaty. These are the people you can count on to grind and do the work necessary with a positive attitude.

There is a problem in the workforce today with "messengers."

Messengers are people who simply pass information around from person to person without ever solving problems, doing the work, or taking the required action. They are a major issue in many large companies and the reason why "middle management" has such a bad reputation.

Messengers operate like this:

A group of managers has a meeting and identifies a major problem. Those managers then leave the meeting and pass the problem and the solution to their underlings, who then pass the problem and the solution to even more underlings.

The people who end up with the problem then identify nuances, bring ideas, talk and think about more solutions, and plan a meeting with management. It goes around and around.

You might have experienced this yourself if you've worked for a decent-size organization. Everybody talks and plans and passes messages, but no one actually steps up to do the work and make the necessary changes. It is a disaster.

As the size of your organization increases, the likelihood that people become messengers increases. And then before you know it, you have an entire layer of management inside your company made up of people who send emails all day without doing any actual work.

It is on *you* to keep this from happening. And it is on you to remove the people who aren't willing to do the work.

I find myself, very often, stating directly to key members of my team, "I don't want you to delegate this. It is important, and I need you to solve this problem yourself. Can you do the work here?"

When we discover serious problems, I put my best people on them. And I'm not afraid to get my own hands dirty and do the work either. When my employees see this, it rubs off. And the good news is that the people who aren't willing to get their hands dirty don't last at my companies.

The Deal-Breakers

So how do we spot the losers? What behaviors are nonstarters? What are the deal-breakers? Here is my list:

Morally Unsound Individuals

Lying, stealing, and cheating are unforgivable to me—there are no second chances here. The minute I figure out somebody is not following the rules and laws of the game, they are cut out of my company and my circle.

Pessimists

Pessimists approach every problem, stressful situation, and difficulty with a negative attitude.

They think of the reasons why something can't be done before they think of the reasons why it can. They complain. They blame other people. They bring others down and make people miserable.

Entrepreneurship is hard, but doing hard things with negative people is a nightmare. Do not let this sickness infect your company or your life. It is contagious and will spread like wildfire if you let it in.

The truth:

Pessimists sound smart. Optimists make money.

Manipulators

A very large portion (I'd guess more than 25 percent) of the population consists of people who manipulate and play head games with other people to get what they want.

Customers who bully you to fleece you out of money. Bosses who use tricks and tactics to fool you into doing what serves them but not you. Partners who make mistakes or poor decisions and spin the situation to be somebody else's fault. Spouses who use fear and emotional abuse to manipulate their husbands or wives into doing what they want.

These people do not have your best interest in mind. They are selfish and destructive.

Do not let them in your business or your life.

People Who Gossip

Gossip is the act of talking bad about people who are not in your presence with other people who are. It is destructive and contagious. If it seeps into your company or your life, it will take hold and spread. It will foster resentment and jealousy. It will make everyone in your family or your organization critical of one another. It will make your company weaker, and it will make your people care less about each other. It will destroy your culture.

People who gossip about others around you will gossip about you around others.

I have a zero-tolerance policy around gossip, and I make that clear to my team every time it shows itself. I never talk negatively about people who are not there. I never spread stories about people's lives.

Make this a habit and it will pay off over time.

People with a "Status Quo" Mindset

There are two types of people in the world:

1. People who are always building, growing, and looking to improve themselves.
2. People who are content and always working to make sure things don't get worse.

Most entrepreneurs fall into the first camp. Most exceptional athletes fall into the first camp. Most successful people in general fall into the first camp.

The majority of people, however, fall into the second camp.

They get home from work and zone out in front of a screen until they need to go back to work. They don't work hard to improve in many areas of life—hobbies, relationships, business, health, fitness, and more.

Make sure you have a healthy balance of driven people who are interested in growing and getting uncomfortable. They will support you and push you to improve and do more with this life you have.

Chapter 10

How to Find High-Performing People

I hang around a decent country club in Athens, Georgia. Many of the people there have gotten opportunities not because of competence or a long interview process but because of proximity.

They just happened to be in the circle when the opportunity came around. They were in the group chat. Or the golf group. Or their name came up in conversation.

You can build a reasonably powerful network simply by being in the club. Knowing people. But this isn't approachable advice for everyone.

How do you get into a nice country club if you can't afford it? How do you make friends there once you are in?

Who you know only gets you so far. And even then, you have to depend on sheer luck to get opportunities, which only come around every so often. Lucky for you, this isn't the most powerful way to build a network.

> **Cold hard truth:**
> It isn't about who you know. It is about who knows you and what you know how to do.

Most people network all wrong. They go to a networking event and walk up to every single person with one goal in mind: I need to figure out how this person can help *me*. Or they fire off cold emails with one goal: I have to get this person to help *me* with a problem I'm having.

What can you do for ME? How can you help ME? ME, ME, ME, ME, ME.

News flash: Everyone in this world is selfish.

They are thinking about themselves and how they can potentially advance their own lives, businesses, organizations, earning potential, or relationships.

That doesn't mean people are constantly looking to take advantage of others—no crabs in a bucket in your business!—but they are looking for win-win scenarios where both parties benefit. The key party is *them*. If *they* don't benefit, they are not interested.

So when you network with your hand out asking for generosity, it is simply not effective. That is why nothing much comes from those networking events where college students shake hands with one another with the me, me, me attitude.

So how *do* you network?

I have some inconvenient news:

You have to do the work and get good at something *before* your network will truly grow. You have to be able to benefit *other people*.

So what does that mean? You build something! You become an expert at something. You develop skills. You make money. You learn to operate a business. You become a master in a certain niche. You become *the* person other people need to talk to when they have questions about a certain thing.

This isn't good news, I know.

Wait, I have to do something else before I can network? I have to become successful in my own right first? That sounds hard. And not very fun. Where is the hack?

News flash:

There is no hack.

Remember when we talked about adding value first? In order to network effectively, you have to bring something to the table. Yes, it is hard, and unfortunately there are no shortcuts.

I know because I went to the college networking events with a selfish attitude. I ran around looking for people who could help me. And it did nothing for me. No one answered my calls. No one took my meetings. But now my network is exceptional. I have access to a bunch of people in all different specialties. People who run multimillion-dollar companies. People who are massively successful in all different verticals. Experts in their fields.

How did I do it?

I became somebody worth knowing.

I built a company. I sold that company. I became an expert in the self-storage business and the international hiring business. I made money. I hired a bunch of people. I became somebody people thought they ought to know because I could probably help them out.

And here is the secret:

People are eager to help people who could potentially return the favor someday.

Remember what I said about selling? That your business isn't about you and what you need? The same thing applies to getting to know other people. Networking, recruiting, hiring—it's all about your ability to add value. If you become a person who can help others, other people are much more likely to help you. Become worth knowing. Focus on your craft. Learn how to manage people. Build that capital and operational ability and watch your network take care of itself.

Recruiting

I have a saying in business:

ABR. Always. Be. Recruiting.

Great entrepreneurs are always hunting for talented people.

At family gatherings, they spend time getting a look into the minds of their relatives and thinking about potential overlap. At local restaurants, they watch people work and see how competent they are at their jobs. At the golf course, they ask people about their experience with certain companies and assess their skills. When they buy from certain vendors, they evaluate how good somebody is at sales or relationship management. They ask probing questions to get a feel for how someone thinks or how they might solve problems.

Great entrepreneurs are also selling these talented people on what they have to offer.

As you recruit, you have to offer win-win scenarios in which you can provide more opportunity, more money, or a better working environment for talented people. You have to make somebody else's life better to attract the right person to your organization.

I have a theory on recruiting:

Ten percent of people are looking for something new. They are either unemployed or unhappy with their current job. They want to quit, and they are actively looking for a new job, applying online, and telling people they are open to work.

At the other end of the spectrum, 10 percent of people are in career nirvana. They would not leave their current position even if an amazing opportunity landed in their lap. They are perfectly happy and extremely well compensated. They love their work environment. Everything is perfect. These people cannot be recruited no matter how good you are.

The 80 percent in the middle—the people who are not actively looking but not perfectly happy—is where you will find the real talent.

The best people out there already have jobs where they are thriving. They are paid well, and they have bosses who really don't want to lose them. They are not unemployed. They are not actively looking for jobs. They may not have the perfect job, but they aren't going to apply to your listing on Indeed or LinkedIn.

Your job as an entrepreneur is to go find these people and convince them to trust you and join your mission because it would make *their* life better.

The most talented person I've ever hired was a buddy. I spent three years selling him on quitting his job in banking and joining my company. I gave him a chance to have more flexibility and control over his schedule and work on more exciting stuff for more long-term upside.

The best salesman I ever hired went to high school with me and was making $200,000 a year selling windows door-to-door. I set him up with a plan to make more money with less travel. He jumped at the opportunity.

The list goes on and on and on.

Notice the pattern?

All of these people had jobs.

All of these people were selfishly, and rightfully, prioritizing their own lives when they decided to come work for me. All of them chose me because I gave them more of what they wanted and improved their career prospects. All because I had my ear to the ground in everyday life.

I was hunting.

For a lot of positions, I recruit in standard ways. I post jobs. I ask my employees for referrals, and I compensate them for referrals that materialize. I interview ten people and hire the best one. It is a tedious process, and you can read about it in any book.

But a lot of my recruiting isn't standard because I am always looking for talent and going out and trying to find it.

I was in a Walmart parking lot in 2014 in Ithaca, New York, at about 8:00 p.m.

It was cold as hell, icy and dark. My girlfriend at the time (now wife) was inside picking up some supplies, and I was on my phone answering emails in my truck.

Out of the corner of my eye, I noticed someone running through the lot.

When I glanced up, I saw he was clean-cut and had a blue vest on—he worked for Walmart. He was rounding up carts, but not in the normal Walmart way. This guy was *hustling*.

He was practically sprinting when every employee I have ever seen at Walmart seemed to walk as slow as physically possible. Why would they hustle? They are getting paid by the hour. There is zero motivation to move quickly. And they are paid near minimum wage.

Before this guy, I had *never* seen a Walmart employee move quickly. Never. This was weird.

After the guy had gotten a bunch of carts, he pushed them full speed back toward the entrance. A piece of trash blew across his path at that very moment, and while pushing the carts he bent down, picked up the garbage, jammed it in his back pocket, and carried on.

I was shocked.

Not only was he moving quickly, but he clearly cared about his job enough to pick up trash in the parking lot. That wasn't in his job description, I was sure of it.

So I made my move.

I acted as if I were walking into the store and made sure our paths crossed. "Wow, man! What's the hurry?"

"The high school basketball game will let out in about twenty minutes, and we'll get swarmed with customers. My manager called in sick, and my co-worker is on break, so I need to make sure we have enough carts for the people who will show up here in a few minutes!"

This guy cared and had a sense of urgency. That automatically put him in the top 5 percent of humans.

"Awesome work," I replied. "I own a moving company in town, and I'm looking to hire people like you. If you have any friends looking for work, we pay $18 an hour, and we do a ton of work at the college, so it's a really fun environment. Here's my card—have anyone you know email me, and we can chat."

I knew he was making $12 an hour.

I also wasn't looking for his friends, but I said it that way to take the pressure off the conversation.

He emailed me three hours later, and we spoke the next morning.

I hired him that afternoon, and he ended up working four seasons with my company and being one of the best hires we ever made. He traveled for me from city to city and ended up managing several locations.

A lot of business owners get stuck in a loop complaining that they can't find good people. This is nothing more than an excuse and a cop-out.

Great people are all over the place if you know where and how to look.

If you notice the communication skills of the lady running the counter and dealing with chaos at a hotel, give her your card. If you see the hardworking bartender with awareness slinging drinks and taking orders for hours without getting impatient, give him your card. It's as simple as that.

You can't teach certain things, and as a business owner I'm always on the lookout for people with these characteristics. It works.

Starbucks does a phenomenal job recruiting and training folks but doesn't pay them much. Enterprise Rent-A-Car has an unbelievable recruiting engine, and somehow they get the most competent go-getters for $15 an hour. I've even handed cards to Target employees I see killing it behind the checkout counter.

No matter where you live or what your business does, I bet you come face-to-face with more than twenty potential employees on an average day running errands around town.

These are the folks you want on your team.

Friends, Family, and Hunting

Conventional wisdom says to *never* hire friends or family.

I'm not so sure about that.

Trust is critical, and a high level of that is built in with family members. Knowing how someone thinks, talks, and reacts to problems is very important. You can get a look at this kind of thing with your relatives and friends and know in advance if it would be likely to work out or not.

I know because I've hired more than ten folks from my direct network of family and friends.

My uncle was the first project manager we hired in self-storage development. My good friend is now our VP of Sales. My partner's childhood friend was our first controller. My best friend in college opened up a branch for us at Indiana University. A friend's sister now runs a division in our real estate company. My partner's first cousin opened a branch of my first company at the University of Illinois. A buddy from the track team launched our business in Philadelphia. One of my partner's childhood friends opened a branch for us at the University of Iowa. I hired a high school buddy to head up acquisitions for my real estate company. The CFO at my real estate company (and arguably the best hire I've ever made) was my girlfriend's roommate's boyfriend after college in Boston. I founded a company with my father. My partner in my real estate company and my student storage business was a college friend, co-captain on the track team, and housemate.

I drank beer with all of these people. I got to know them in advance. I worked out with them. I competed with them. I explored with them and vacationed with them.

Friends and family are great hires because you have a preview of their habits, thought processes, moral compass, energy levels, and positivity. You know if they are complainers or gossipers. You know how they think about business or problems from previous conversations.

If you are an excellent communicator and good at managing expectations, this can work really well.

The key is to outline the negatives in the process just as you would with anyone else. Make sure the person taking the job knows it might not work forever, that you might need to part ways and want to do so without hard feelings, and that they won't be the recipient of special treatment.

If you're not good at reading people and figuring out who might be a fit at your company, then hiring friends and family is not for you. If you're not good at having difficult conversations and communicating important but uncomfortable things, this is not for you. If you're prone to burning bridges or getting in disagreements with folks, this is not for you.

I've fired several of my close friends. I've dissolved partnerships. I've had a good buddy cry in my arms after letting him go.

It is brutal.

But if you treat people fairly and you don't screw them over, you can maintain the relationship. I always have. I'm proud to say that I have never had a falling-out with a friend or family member who worked for me. I've fired them, and they have quit, but I have never had a falling-out.

I know this isn't the norm. Many people are not good at managing these relationships and handling them in an effective way. But if you can walk the tightrope, I highly recommend hiring people you have previous experience with.

In 2021, my real estate company was growing fast. I needed somebody to help me onboard new properties and deal with the new tenants, new leases, collecting payment, and getting us set up with a new software system. Every property we bought involved onboarding several hundred tenants and getting them on our systems.

I spent a few days thinking hard about who might be a good fit.

I realized that teachers are amazingly organized, are great writers and communicators, and generally work hard.

The pandemic also changed everything for them. They were still getting paid about $40,000 per year in my area, but remote work had turned their jobs into a fiasco. They spent hours and hours messaging parents, trying to keep up with thirty kids and their assignments, and more.

Generally speaking, the money teachers were making was not worth the headache they were enduring (and are still enduring) in the school systems.

I put the word out among my management team asking if anybody knew any teachers who were unhappy with their jobs. One of my managers instantly told us that his sister was a third-grade teacher but looking to get out of the profession altogether.

So I interviewed her, gave her a computer literacy assessment that tests general speed and typing efficiency, which she passed with flying colors. Then I offered her a job and she accepted.

We paid her $50,000, which was a $10,000 annual raise, and let her work from home. She has been a phenomenal asset to my business and still works with us today.

It turns out that if you can manage thirty nine-year-olds, managing thirty-nine-year-olds is a piece of cake.

Get out a piece of paper or open your computer. I have another assignment for you:

First, make a list of the skills you need at your company.

Is it sales? Is it communication? Is it critical thinking and leadership? Is it management? Is it organization?

Now think about what jobs these people currently have in your town.

Are they doing what you need them to do today but for a competitor? Or would you be training somebody from scratch and looking for certain skills?

The last step:

How could you get in front of these people and approach them about a job opportunity? Could it be through your network? Or do you need to go out and hunt? What could you offer them that they don't have in their current role? How could you convince them to join you?

What you're doing here is building a profile of the perfect employee. You are painting a picture of exactly who you need, where they are, and how you could recruit them. This is a very valuable exercise and will help you make the right hire.

In the next chapter, we'll get into the weeds on making that hire and managing your early employees.

Chapter 11

Hiring—The Key to Ultimate Leverage

One of the mistakes I've made again and again is waiting too long to hire for a critical position.

When I first started Storage Squad in 2011, my partner and I did everything. We drove trucks, invoiced customers, answered the phone, leased the warehouses, rented the equipment, answered emails, called every upset customer, and more.

We had no time to focus on hiring, training, selling new customers, marketing initiatives, or any of the important, high-leverage things that would have grown our business. We didn't have time to expand to new regions or chase talent. We didn't understand that hiring overseas was even a possibility, and we couldn't afford a full-time, U.S.-based employee for more than $40,000 annually. So we did it all.

Our business was growing—we had tapped into a proven opportunity, and we had cash flow—but I talked myself out of making more hires than I care to admit. "We don't need to outlay the capital for this," I thought. "I'm not sure we have a full-time job yet. I can just keep doing these tasks myself. We'll have more money at the end of the year if we spend less money on people."

Don't do this.

I'd end up pulling the trigger eventually after a lot of unnecessary stress. Then, a week after making a hire I was sure we didn't need and couldn't afford, they were already adding so much value that I wondered how I had lived without them and kicked myself for waiting so long.

If you're spending too much of your time doing the work required to actually keep your business running, it is time to hire. If you're spending too much of your time doing work that you could pay somebody $20 an hour to do, it is time to hire.

Basically, whenever you find that *you* are the bottleneck keeping your company from growing, it's time to hire.

There are no answers or steadfast rules. Every situation is different. It requires a bit of figuring it out as you go. It requires a lot of practice. It requires making mistakes and changing course. I've hired hundreds of people in my life. Many of them have worked out. A lot of them haven't. But here are the best practices, tips, and strategies that I've developed over the years. Let's get started.

The First Hire Is the Hardest

Trusting somebody with your business, your livelihood, your customers, and your reputation is scary.

What if they mess up? How can I afford them? When is the right time? What do I pay them?

These kinds of questions will keep you running in place... forever.

One of the biggest myths of running your own business is that you *have* to do every job yourself for as long as you can take it.

It's a ridiculous badge of honor among entrepreneurs, but at a certain point it becomes too much. And more important, poor customer service and missed calls impact your bottom line. Good enough ends up not being good enough.

There are three types of hires:

The administrators do repeatable tasks on a computer. They answer phones and send invoices. They handle the bookkeeping and keep things organized. They do takeoffs or create proposals.

The technicians provide service to your customers. They do the day-to-day work. Many times they are manual laborers in home service businesses, or they work remotely in a lot of agencies or companies.

The managers are the glue that holds it together. They make decisions on the direction of the company. They explore new initiatives and drive growth. They lead people. They set employee schedules. They interview, hire and fire, and make key decisions operationally. They are the highest paid and hardest to replace.

It almost always makes sense for the first hire to be either an admin or a technician while you, the owner, free up time to do more high-level work.

An example:

My friend runs a consulting business, and she was working more than fifty hours a week, struggling to keep up with invoicing, customer service, collections, and other simple tasks while also providing her core service, sales consulting.

She couldn't handle more business, because she was spending thirty hours a week billing time to her clients and the other twenty on administrative work.

Her first hire was an admin assistant from the Philippines for $800 per month to help with client scheduling, emails, travel booking, billing, and more.

She bills her clients more than $300 per hour for her sales consulting. An expense of $800 per month allowed her to bill an extra five or ten hours per week with ease *and* actually work less.

My very first entrepreneurial endeavor began when I was thirteen years old and I hired my first employee when I was fourteen.

My father helped me secure a lawn-mowing job in Tell City, Indiana, for his boss, who owned a lot of retail and apartments in the town.

He sat me down at the kitchen table and set up a lease program on the family truck and zero-turn lawn mower so I could use both. I wasn't old enough to drive, so the original plan was to pay my mom $10 per trip to town and she would drop me off and run errands.

The job was difficult in the Indiana summers. I cried on the first day in ninety-eight-degree heat.

I had several years' experience mowing the family lawn, so my father had simply dropped me off to do the job. But I mowed over about 100 pieces of trash and turned them into 100,000 pieces of trash by chopping them all into little pieces.

When my father came back to check on me half an hour later, I was mowing along and creating this disaster in real time. He pulled me aside and gave me constructive feedback and made me begin picking up the trash.

It took three hours. I cried and told him that I wanted to quit!

He put his arm around me and gave me a cold Gatorade. He very wisely told me I couldn't quit until my first paycheck came. We got home after a long day, and I faxed an invoice for $120 to the customer.

A check showed up two weeks later. I was hooked from then on and haven't had a real job since.

My mother got tired of our arrangement, so I was forced to hire a high school kid with a driver's license and mowing experience.

I went to the high school hallway at Perry Central Jr.-Sr. High School and slipped a handwritten, copied flyer inside each of the two hundred lockers for juniors and seniors. The flyer said "Lawn Mowing Job. $12.50 an hour" along with my phone number.

I found a great employee quickly, and he turned three and a half hours of work into two hours and 15 minutes. With travel I could do the job door to door in three hours. I began to make real money—north of $40 an hour after all my expenses—at age fourteen.

I added more jobs and worked more hours as I got older but never grew beyond one employee.

I went to college at eighteen years old with $40,000 in my bank account and owned my own paid-off vehicle.

A note:

Hiring employees is expensive.

As a rule of thumb, you want to be able to bill a customer two to three times what you are paying an employee to deliver the work. That means $50–$75 per hour to make a healthy margin if you are paying an employee $20–$25 an hour. It may feel like a lot, but between employment taxes, benefits, overhead, and lost time due to training, vacation, idle time, and travel, three times is often the multiple to maintain healthy margins.

Back to lawn care as an example:

If you are paying your crew members $20 per hour, a one-hour lawn for two employees should cost a customer $80 to $120 per visit.

You might not think this is possible.

Why would anyone pay $120 for me to mow a lawn that takes two people one hour?

But they will. You have to build trust, show professionalism, and deliver a great service. You can work on your sales and marketing to achieve this rate or get into a better business if it isn't possible in your area in a certain industry.

Now I have an assignment for you:

I built a spreadsheet where you can experiment with the wage you pay your employees, the price you charge your customers, and your profit margin when it is all said and done.

Download the sheet at **sweatystartup.com/wages** and play around with it.

Input what you charge, what you pay, and how long the job takes. Take some time to experiment and figure out *exactly* how much you need to charge a customer to operate at a 50 percent labor margin and a 30 percent overall margin.

You might be pleasantly surprised that you have the revenue to hire someone today, or you might be discouraged that you don't. Either way, now you know.

A Low-Risk Way to Start

Nowadays, computers are where real productivity happens.

That's how you send proposals for new work, follow up with clients, collect money, and more. When a small business owner is away from their computer, their business isn't growing and they are likely falling behind. So whether it's your first hire or your second, in almost all situations an administrative assistant to take care of 20 to 30 percent of your tasks for $12,000 to $15,000 per year is critical.

Here's my big secret:

About 80 percent of the more than three hundred employees across my portfolio are located in Latin America, South Africa, eastern Europe, and the Philippines.

They are exceptionally hardworking, competent decision makers, and I pay them about 80 percent less than I would U.S. employees. In my companies, overseas employees do anything that can be done from a computer. Their English skills are incredible, and their work ethic is unmatched.

The average starting wage is $800 per month or less than $4.60 per hour.

Relatively speaking, these people earn a phenomenal amount of money because the cost of living in their home countries is so low.

A lot of people argue that hiring abroad is anti-American. I totally disagree.

First of all, Americans have an insatiable desire for low-cost goods—that is why they shop at Walmart (where 98 percent of the goods are manufactured overseas) and buy iPhones that were assembled for $3 per hour. Large companies have been outsourcing for sixty-five years, but small businesses aren't allowed to do the same?

The second part of the equation is that there simply aren't enough Americans willing to do the work to assemble our iPhones, manufacture our steel, answer our phones, and more. The unemployment rate in the United States has never been an issue—America is the wealthiest country in the world and consumes much more than it produces. So whether you like it or not, we *need* the help of overseas employees to deliver everything we want to consume.

Hiring overseas makes for an incredibly low-risk hire. Instead of committing to $50,000 per year with another $7,000 worth of taxes and benefits, you can get a full-time employee for 80 percent less.

That is literally an extra $45,000, or $22.50 for every working hour, back in your pocket that you can invest in your business and your growth.

Another very surprising thing:

I also hire high-level employees overseas. We've hired exceptionally talented managers in Colombia, salespeople in South Africa, financial analysts in Brazil, operations leads in Mexico, software engineers in Argentina, web developers in the Philippines, designers in Peru, and more.

These are roles for which we would pay more than $100,000 in the United States, but these overseas hires start at $1,500 per month.

I have several folks from South Africa and Latin America in particular who run whole divisions of my companies. One individual, Andres, who I hired out of Colombia in 2021 at a $1,500 per month starting salary, will likely become the CEO of one of my companies within the next five years.

If you'd like to get a glimpse of this talent and meet my team, please visit **sweatystartup.com/talent** and watch the video.

Where do you find the people?

I use Somewhere.com, a recruiting company that I also own, to find the talent for me. They vet and interview the candidates first, then they let you interview and make an offer. They guarantee the hire for six months as a part of their fee, so if there are any problems, they will find you somebody else. No pressure at all to use

Somewhere.com to recruit your talent, but if you'd like to learn more, email me at **nick@sweatystartup.com** and I can introduce you to my team and get you a $500 discount off the recruiting fee.

From HVAC companies to home inspection companies to internet companies, I have recommended that several friends hire overseas talent through Somewhere.com. Virtually all of them have called me or told me less than three months later that it has been a game changer for them, and they plan to make many more hires.

I'm not surprised because hiring overseas talent has been a total game changer for me and my businesses. I can run my real estate private equity company with forty-five employees for $1.3 million a year while my competitors spend more than $4 million to staff a similar team stateside.

It allows us to grow faster, operate with less risk, and hire more people ahead of revenue. It allows us to win.

Alignment

At the end of every interview I frame a simple scenario, and it goes like this:

Let's pretend we're on this video call or in this office five years from now for an annual check-in. You tell me that you *love* your job and you love this company. Your team is great. Your boss is great and you really enjoy your day-to-day work. Put yourself in that moment five years from now. Tell me about your ideal world. What do you love about your job? What position are you in? How much money are you making and what does your team look like?

For better or for worse, the responses will tell you everything you need to know about what the person you are about to hire *truly wants* and if it will be a good fit.

The goal of this conversation is to get to the bottom of somebody's real motivations. You will learn what they want out of a job. You'll learn what their goals really are.

Recently, I had a candidate for a management position tell me something that didn't line up with their role during this part of the interview.

"I don't get energy from people problems, so I would like to be working with a small team and adding a lot of value to the customers I work with. I feel empowered and rewarded when I finish a productive day's work and succeed at it. I want to make customers happy. And it is also very important for me to enjoy the people I'm working with every day. I don't like dealing with problems that aren't straightforward. I am an analytical person who uses data to make decisions. I don't like drama or dealing with people's emotions."

This was for a management position that involved dealing with people. Managing their problems. Setting schedules and hiring and firing people. And all of the complexity that comes with that. The answer to my final question told me that this was not a fit.

A quick reminder:

It isn't only about you and what you want in an employee. What the employee wants and desires matters an awful lot. After all, you're asking them to devote forty hours a week for a good chunk of their career to you.

What skills do they want to develop? What roles do they want to grow into?

And most important:

Can your company deliver? Can you deliver? Can you give the employee what they want so that they are happy and fulfilled at work?

If you can't, it will not work.

There is nothing worse for either of you than leading an employee down a career path for your own benefit when you know that they'll eventually become unhappy and leave, so it's best to align expectations early so all parties can find a job mutually beneficial.

What Competent People Want

I spend a lot of time asking my high-performing friends what frustrates them about their work environments.

What do you dislike about your boss? What drives you crazy and causes stress at work? What makes you feel unproductive?

These conversations have taught me a lot about what to do and even more about what not to do. And I've used these insights to design a place where high-performing employees want to work.

As a result, I have very little turnover. I've created compensation plans to keep people around for the long haul, and I do the right things in my organization to reduce stress and make it enjoyable.

While there are many details about hiring and recruiting that will be specific to you and your business, I've found three key strategies that will help any entrepreneur retain competent people and create a great work environment for them:

Structure Is Good

Business books, podcasts, and social media will tell you that employees want freedom above all else. They want to make their own schedules. They want to solve problems on their own and work in a way that works for them. They want autonomy, flexibility, and a dynamic environment.

This is total bullshit.

Employees, even the highest performers, want structure.

Ninety-nine percent of people prefer to be told what to do and how to win. Straightforward solutions, benchmarks, and a clear path forward make them feel confident in you and the business. They don't like dealing with ambiguous situations or uncomfortable conversations. They are actively trying to *avoid* chaos.

If they wanted chaos, they would be entrepreneurs.

I've made this mistake before. Believing that everyone thinks like me and enjoys making decisions with incomplete information, figuring things out as they go, and putting out fires. This is the natural mistake of the entrepreneur:

We assume everyone sees the world the way we do and thrives on the same type of uncertainty.

The truth is that people who have jobs want to be set up to succeed. They want to know what to expect. They want to know that if they do a certain thing well, the results will follow. They want to do a good job, be recognized for their work, and get paid every other week. They want to have happy customers and happy co-workers. This can't exist in an environment of chaos.

So establish structure and rules. *Tell people what to do.*

And then hold them accountable for doing it.

Make Decisions and Changes Quickly

My neighbor in Boston totally crushed it at work.

He was an extremely competent in-house attorney for an insurance company who regularly met unbelievable deadlines and did the work of three people. He was also very improvement focused, always looking for ways to make the business, its processes, and the lives of its employees and customers just a little bit better.

Many weekends, we sat around talking business over beer, and he told me about all of his ideas. New customer management software. A better way to organize policies. Revamping the structure of the company to better serve the customers and remove inefficiency.

Unfortunately, he also complained about the outcome of all his ideas.

He regularly brought solutions to his bosses, and at first they talked a big game. They agreed that the issues he pointed out were important and that the company needed to innovate to stay on the cutting edge.

And then nothing would happen. No implementation. No decisions.

What did I learn from him?

When high performers know what needs to be done to improve things but are stuck doing things the old, stressful way, it eats away at their souls and spirits. It creates a culture of resentment. They will be gone before you know it.

My neighbor quit that job a few months later and went to work for a real estate developer who was open-minded and aggressive. He is happier than ever.

The lesson:

You don't need to take action on every piece of advice or idea an employee brings, but if you do nothing at all when your team knows there is a better way, your days are numbered. Make decisions quickly and make things happen!

Move fast. Change is good. If you aren't improving, you are dying.

This is how you keep your high performers happy.

Surround Your A Players with A Players

A few years ago, I got an email from one of my social media followers who hated her job.

She was an account manager at an insurance firm. The buck stopped with her.

If her clients weren't happy, she had to make it right or she would lose the account and lose a chunk of her income. But she was surrounded by C players who were terrible at their jobs.

That meant picking up the slack for them when they made mistakes. It meant cleaning up their messes and often even *doing* their work. She couldn't spend her time doing what she did best—the client management—and it made her life as a high performer miserable.

She had gone to her boss many times to complain about the incompetence around her. Telling them she needed to hire new people and that the company should get rid of the poor performers.

But her boss never did anything. They let it slide. And her life continued to be miserable until she quit and went somewhere else.

The golden rule of retaining A players:

If you surround them with C players, they will be miserable.

If you do not have the courage or willingness to fire incompetent people, they will be miserable. If they are stuck picking up the slack for people who are not good at their jobs, they will be miserable.

In corporate America, people can hide. People can do zero work for years and years and get promoted because they show up on time every day. High performers hate working for these giant corporations because incompetence is tolerated.

Do not let your company turn into this.

I was once on a phone call with Chris Powers, one of my mentors, complaining about an employee's performance and talking about how it was impossible to help them improve. I had given them countless chances, always thinking that if I just worked harder to communicate or did better with training, it wouldn't happen again. Only to be let down.

"Why haven't you let this person go?"

I pretended not to know the answer, but of course I did. It was a tough labor market, and I knew it would be a lot of work and stress *for me* to pick up the slack while *also* making another hire. I would have to train another person even though I was already really busy. Plus it's scary and uncomfortable to fire someone. No fun at all.

He then said something I'll never forget:

"Your company's performance will fall to the level of incompetence that you tolerate. The choice is simple. Fire your low performers or watch your high performers walk away. If you tolerate C players, your company will become a C-level organization in the blink of an eye."

This turned out to be one of the best pieces of advice I have ever received and I live by it to this day.

Fire your low performers or watch your high performers walk away. I let that person go the next day, and within a week the entire company was in a better spot. I felt as if a weight had been lifted off my shoulders. The stress just vanished.

Making hard decisions and letting people go are required if you are an entrepreneur. If you want to maintain the health of your company and look out for the well-being of everybody, you must be willing to show poor performers the door.

High performers show themselves very quickly—I can tell in

a matter of weeks or days if somebody will be a superstar—but it generally takes much longer for a poor performer to become obvious.

If you want to be happy and successful, you should accept something as fact:

People do not change.

Bad customers don't get better. Poor employees don't improve. Unreliable people don't become reliable.

Accept people the way they are and find a place for them in your organization where they can thrive or let them go. Do not try to change them. Do not hope they will change. You damn sure can't bet your company or your well-being on people changing. If you do, you'll end up broke, frustrated, and surrounded by people who have made the decision to remain the same.

I've fired nearly a hundred people in my career.

It never gets easier. I always dread it. It is always emotional and complicated. My advice is to cut to the chase, deliver the news, provide a very generous severance, and help them find their next position that is a better fit for their skills.

But it isn't fair to you, your team, or the employee to keep them around in a job they can't do well.

A company is not a family. It is a sports team.

If somebody is not producing, you need to muster up the courage and move on.

Swallow Your Pride

Hiring will humble you and toy with your emotions.

Last year one of my companies was growing fast, and we were

stressed to the max. We needed some key talent, and I was on the hunt to get it. An important member of my management team was in tears during one of our weekly all-hands meetings.

Things were too busy. We couldn't deliver. So we made the decision within a few minutes that we needed to hire and we needed to hire fast.

My co-founder started a search and found the perfect guy within a week. He had experience, the technical background, and the industry-specific knowledge.

He wasn't happy with his current gig, so I knew we could get him and it would help our company reach the next level. The interviews went great. The team loved him. We floated a compensation package, and he agreed.

I thought it was a done deal.

We sent the formal offer and received radio silence for four days. I called him, but he didn't answer. Then we got an email from him that he was declining the job because his employer had offered him more money. My team was upset.

We went back to the drawing board and began the search all over again.

Then something odd happened.

A week later, he came back saying he had messed up. "Is the offer still good?" he asked. "Can I have another chance?" We learned later he had gotten into an argument with his current employer and quit a few days after striking his new deal.

I really, really wanted to tell him no.

The entire situation rubbed me the wrong way, and I was sure it was a red flag. His flip-flopping was a sign of more drama to come and poor decision making. So we called a team meeting.

I told everyone that I thought we should just move on, but my co-founder insisted that we swallow our pride and make the hire. I accepted the blow to my ego and eventually agreed.

We re-extended the offer and he accepted, coming on board a few days later.

To make a long story short, he has been one of the best hires we have ever made. He rebuilt our tech stack. Changed the way we delivered our product for the better. Leads a team on improving our processes to this day.

The lesson:

People are unpredictable and hiring is messy and complicated.

They will often make mistakes, and you might occasionally overreact. Being stubborn doesn't get you anywhere and is very likely to set you back. Have an open mind, change your mind often, trust your team, and take some chances on people. They might just surprise you.

Chapter 12

Management and Delegation

When you are an entrepreneur, employees come to you with problems and questions nonstop. How you handle them is what separates the good managers from the poor managers, the effective delegators from the ineffective delegators.

Option 1 is to take over and solve the problem yourself.

This is the easiest way to handle things in the short run. You are the boss, and you are better at solving problems, especially ones related to the business you started. And let's face it:

Sometimes just doing it is much easier than teaching someone in the moment.

Option 2 is to do the work to teach your employee how to solve the problem themselves.

This is the path of most resistance, but it is also key for your long-term success. You could just let the employee off easy and enable their lack of critical thinking, *or* you can challenge them to think (and get a window into how their mind works).

Even though it wasn't always the case, when an employee comes to me now with a question, any question, I always ask them the same exact question in reply.

What would you do and why?

I'll ask leading question after leading question.

What is the goal here? What are the downsides? What are the risks?

This is the process of teaching your employees how to think for themselves. You put the problem back on them so that they can learn to think critically. It creates a teaching moment in which they are forced to exercise their ability to make decisions.

I call this the "monkey on the back" conundrum.

When an employee comes to you with a problem, that problem is a giant monkey on their back. As soon as they describe the problem and ask you how to solve it, the monkey jumps off their back and onto your desk.

It is now your problem. That monkey is yours to look after.

You can send the employee on their way, keep their monkey, and solve their problem. Or you can make sure they walk out of your office with their monkey and a plan to take care of it themselves.

If you take the easy route, which is to keep the monkey and take care of it yourself, you breed an environment within your company in which none of your employees know how to care for their own monkeys. They *always* show up on your desk.

Every single problem ends up being *your* responsibility.

Not only will you always be stressed out, but you'll also end up being the bottleneck inside your business. There will be monkeys lined up outside your door. The hallway outside your office will be like a backed-up pipe full of monkeys.

Business won't be able to continue. Decisions won't get made. Things will be slow. And you will be living a life of hell.

But if you get your employees used to taking care of their own monkeys, two things will happen:

1. The employees will get better at taking care of monkeys.

Eventually, they'll solve problems without coming into your office at all. Your phone will stop ringing. They'll start preventing the problems in the first place. They'll understand the goals of the company and will be good at making their own decisions.

2. You'll learn which employees are great at making decisions.

I generally promote from within because I know how all of my employees think. They ask me questions and bring me their monkeys, and I get a look right into their brains as they think through problems. While I'm asking leading questions, I'm also figuring out who is ready (or eventually will be ready) for the next level.

The sad truth is that most humans aren't nearly as competent at making decisions as you'd like to believe.

It's why the average American has an $1,400 car payment, is obese, is divorced, scrolls TikTok for five hours a day, drinks four beers every day after work, does absolutely nothing to get ahead or try hard to get better at anything, dyes their hair purple, and lives paycheck to paycheck.

The brainpower isn't there.

This process is valuable on so many levels. You learn which employees need to be fired and which ones just don't think about things the right way. You learn which ones should *not* be put in decision-making roles and what their weaknesses are.

But something miraculous will also happen.

About 20 percent of people will show you that they really think about things the right way. They'll make good decision after good decision. When you talk through things with them, you'll be pleasantly surprised by how their minds work.

These folks can then be tasked with making decisions *for you*.

They can be promoted into management roles so the decisions and monkeys come to them. And after years and years of this, you'll end up with other people who can take care of monkeys. You'll have a business that makes you money without your involvement.

The Two Levels of Delegating

Level 1: Delegating Tasks

Once you've hired an employee, the first phase of delegation for any manager or entrepreneur is getting them to do a task for you.

Imagine a lawn care company owner hiring his first employee to run the trimmer. Or a podcaster hiring a virtual assistant in the Philippines to edit their show.

Whether it's your first employee or your five hundredth, delegating even the smallest task can be scary and uncomfortable because you can do it better.

When you first delegate, there will be mistakes. There will be questions. There will be money lost when an employee messes up and breaks something on the job.

But if you can get through the discomfort, if you can minimize mistakes, your life will begin to open up.

By delegating tasks, you're basically buying your time back. Somebody else works one hour and it saves you forty-five minutes. You are paying them $15 and in return you get forty-five minutes of your life back. This is the first form of time leverage.

Then, once you get good at delegating the little stuff, you can start to delegate the big stuff. But if delegating low-skill tasks is uncomfortable, delegating higher-skilled tasks is really uncomfortable. So you have to practice with the first level of delegation:

Tasks.

With tasks, there are no decisions that need to be made. We're just talking about repeatable actions that someone can learn and then do over and over and over again to complete a function of your business.

You can run a very large, profitable business with only this level of delegation. I have friends who do it. Their people do all of the repetitive work, but all the decisions still come to them. All problems still come to them. They are stressed, and they work a lot.

They can't play golf without answering a phone call or responding to a message. If they go on vacation, nothing moves forward. Everything just limps along or stops.

If you can delegate tasks, you are ahead of 90 percent of people. You can achieve time leverage and make hundreds of thousands (or even millions in the right business) per year. But eventually you'll become a bottleneck inside your business.

And that's when you'll realize that delegation isn't just about tasks—it's also about delegating decisions.

Level 2: Delegating Decisions

Delegating decisions is the key to truly running a successful company that can grow beyond you.

When you delegate decisions, you're not only giving power to your employees, you're also transferring some of the mental load that comes along with being an entrepreneur.

Your employees can quote the jobs and name the price. They can select the vendor and sign contracts. They can interview and make hiring decisions. They can decide on compensation and bonuses. They can meet with investors. They can negotiate with bankers. They can be an extension of you.

And most important, they can solve problems.

The first major breakthrough in my business occurred in the spring of 2014, our third year in business. We were having dinner with our management team on a Friday night during our busy season.

One of our team members started telling a war story about how an employee had quit that day and abandoned one of our delivery vehicles in the middle of the city.

Before that night, I would have gotten a phone call.

Nick, what should I do?

But I hadn't gotten a call.

My manager went online, looked in our employee database, sent out a group text using our software, and found another employee who could come in and finish the shift. He even made the decision on the spot to offer the employee who covered a $50 bonus to reward him for showing up and solving problems.

When the employee arrived, he didn't have the schedule or the equipment he needed, so my manager sent that stuff along in another truck that was already heading in that direction.

The entire problem was solved in a matter of about thirty minutes, and I didn't hear a word about it.

My head nearly exploded. Part of me was mad.

Why didn't he call me?

But that feeling was the result of my immaturity at the time. I soon realized that what had happened was going to be a transformational experience for me.

From then on, when urgent questions or emergency calls came in, we encouraged our managers to think about a solution *before* calling us.

At first, it made me nervous going a whole day without dealing with a crisis—our whole business had been dealing with crises until then—but soon enough I felt more relaxed than I had since I'd chalked the first Storage Squad ad at Cornell.

That's because it didn't take long until these decisions started getting delegated everywhere.

For the first time since I started my business, I wasn't the bottleneck.

My Job, Our Job, Your Job

This all sounds great and easy. I'll just hire somebody and tell them what to do. Then I'll send them on their way. Right?

Wrong.

A huge mistake people make is they actually *delegate too fast and too aggressively*.

They tell somebody what to do one time and turn them loose. This actually happens often to higher-level managers who are used to managing teams and running projects. Problems come up, and they dish them off with a Slack message, a phone call, a text, or an email. "Hey, go do this. Thanks."

I once had a manager who did this all the time. The process went something like this:

I'd spot a problem at the company and would get to the bottom of it with a few questions.

For example, I'd be listening to customer service calls at the storage company. Our reps' script would be a bit off, and I'd want to change the order in which they said something. *Let's talk about our discount first, and then let's work into the unit pricing and try to figure out what location they are calling about.*

"Hey, Maria," I'd say. "Let's change this. Can we switch the order?"

"Done," she'd say.

A few weeks later, I'd listen to the calls again, and the order still wasn't right. The reps weren't mentioning the discount first. What happened?

What happened was that my manager didn't follow through, follow up, and give guidance. She simply passed on the message and considered the change implemented.

But in reality, when you delegate, you have to tell an employee what to do, coach them on how to do it, and then follow up with them to make sure they change something about how they are doing their job. It is a process.

My job. Our job. Your job.

First, it is *my* job. Then it is *our* job. Then it is *your* job.

My job is to make sure that you can do the job efficiently and perfectly before I stop working with you. So first I'm going to make it our job and our responsibility. I'm going to hold your hand. I'm going to coach you. I'm going to check your work and listen to the call and make sure it is happening correctly. I'm going to provide feedback. This can take weeks or even months with high-level tasks and decisions.

Then, when I am *finally* comfortable with the way you are performing the job and confident in your continued ability to do it, it is officially *your* job and it is no longer on my plate.

Warning:

Delegation takes follow-up and continued monitoring. If there is no accountability, employees will slip back into easier ways or shortcuts. Running a company is a constant system of checks and balances. Everyone needs to know that if they don't do their jobs the way they need to be done, somebody will find out and they will be approached.

This is how you properly delegate.

So as an entrepreneur, you must understand that delegation is a process. There is hand-holding. You are investing in people. Teaching them things takes time. It doesn't happen overnight.

Spend the time. Do the work. Hold the hand. Answer the questions.

A note on management and communication:

People have extremely short attention spans.

If you talk all day, an employee will retain about fifteen minutes of it. If you write a thousand-word email, an employee will skim it and forget nine hundred words of it. If your training video is twenty minutes long, nobody will watch it.

They may look at you and nod . . . but they aren't paying attention.

Keep it short and simple.

If you can say something in fifteen seconds that it takes others three minutes to say, you will drastically outperform other managers when it comes to delegation. Clear and simple communication, both written and verbal, is a superpower.

Here's how to practice this:
1. Before you hit send, go through your email and remove as many words as possible. Strip it down to the bare bones. No emails over two hundred words ever.
2. Record yourself talking. Get a transcript and edit it. Be ruthless. Cut every word that isn't necessary.

3. Make Loom videos for training purposes and make sure they aren't longer than five minutes each. Loom is the No. 1 tool I use to pass messages and training-related stuff to my employees. If a picture is worth a thousand words, a video of you doing a task on the computer with your talking head floating in the corner must be worth a million.
4. Do *not* make the mistake of recording twenty-minute Loom videos. Record more videos on precise topics and make them short. Less than three minutes if possible.

Clear and concise communication is the ace up your delegation sleeve. Master it and your leverage will increase with your earnings.

Getting Out of the Weeds

Staying in the weeds is comfortable.

But I never had that luxury with any of my businesses.

I came up in entrepreneurship being forced to delegate at all costs. At one point, we operated Storage Squad in twelve states at twenty-five different college campuses. We couldn't be everywhere at once. We couldn't drive over and solve problems. We had no choice but to empower employees on the ground.

When I was running the company during the busy season, I could not leave my computer or disaster would strike. I *had* to focus on the big stuff—the schedules, the staffing, the growth. If I left my computer, I was doing $20-an-hour work driving a truck, loading boxes, organizing a warehouse, and so on.

As we grew, my partner and I used to say that we could not, under any circumstances, leave our computers. If we did, and we started working on urgent stuff instead of important stuff, the business would suffer because we weren't being efficient from an opportunity cost standpoint.

It was a beautiful thing because we got really good at management and delegation.

It was a simple choice. We could stay on our computers, where we were efficient and doing $100-an-hour work, or we could get in the weeds and start doing the $20-an-hour work.

The fact that we had no other option was a blessing.

We had to—we got to—focus on the big stuff.

Do we have enough employees lined up to do the work tomorrow and next week? Have we communicated with them adequately? Are they trained and ready to go?

We asked the important questions instead of being consumed by schedules and pickups and deliveries going on at that very moment.

Many business owners bury their heads in the weeds because it feels productive. There is a level of comfort when you are moving the business forward by laboring or being on the front lines.

But this is a trap.

"I'm too busy to worry about growing the business" is an excuse, and a poor one.

So your final challenge is this:

Go back to chapter 7, find something urgent but not important on your list, and figure out how to delegate it to someone today.

Maybe you'll have to hire someone, maybe you'll have to pass the task off to someone who already works for you, or maybe you'll ultimately decide that whatever it is isn't really as necessary as you thought and no one will ever do that job again. Whatever it is, it's time to start making space for what comes next.

Know this:

The relationship with your business will change over time. And the bottlenecks will change, too.

In the early days, it might feel impossible to answer the phone and sell new jobs when it takes all your time and energy to deliver your service. Down the road you may be spending too much time talking to investors and bankers to zoom out and think about the market as a whole and make the important decisions required to steer the entire company.

For the most part, staying buried in the weeds just means staying small. But it can also be catastrophic. When you're buried in the weeds, you can miss important warning signs and blind spots can destroy your decision making.

You can miss trends shifting. You don't have time to research and pay attention to your competitors and how they are innovating. You don't have time to innovate inside your own company and improve operations. And you can fall behind and get passed up. This is one of the many reasons why some business owners still operate with fax machines and phone calls as if it were 1985.

So look at the big picture.

Pull your head out of the weeds. Do the big things that you know need to be done to protect your business and help it grow into the future.

Chapter 13

What Is This All About?

This entire book has been about using entrepreneurship and other tools to make money and grow companies. But ultimately who cares?

How will a sweaty startup really *make you happy?*

Unfortunately, business and financial success is only part of this game. We still wake up every day in the same body with the same issues and the same people around us.

In my opinion, a person needs to be well-rounded and balanced, so there's more to life than just money and your career. There is fitness and physical health. You only get one body—you can't take it with you. There is your mind and your mental health. There are relationships with your friends, your spouse, and your children.

The people around you to share this life are what is important.

Business is fun. It is my calling, and I will always be involved in it.

There are few things in life more enjoyable to me than growing companies. It is so challenging and addictive that it is hard to want to do other things when you're in the thick of it. But ultimately, starting and running a business isn't about the money. It's about having the freedom to do what you want to do when you want to do it.

I have a few more pieces of advice that I wanted to pass along before we close out this book.

Geography

I feel strongly that too many people live where they live because that's where they were born or got a job, not because they actually *want* to live there.

More people should take ownership over their location and move away from home.

In 2017, my wife and I were renting a shitty three-bedroom apartment in Medford, Massachusetts, above an appliance store at 454 Main Street. We stepped around broken washers and dryers to get in the door and walked up many steps to our apartment. We had a four-month-old baby, our first.

On paper, it made perfect sense.

I had been building my student storage business, Storage Squad, in the Boston area since 2014, and my wife was now a stay-at-home mom for the first time. But we were paying $2,500 per month in rent. The winters were long, and we parked on the street. The traffic was horrible. The people weren't friendly. Homes worth buying were more than $500,000 at that time and were forty-five minutes from the city.

So we decided to leave.

My wife was from a small town in upstate New York, and I'm from a small town in southern Indiana. Neither was right for us. So we made a list of things we wanted and didn't show each other our lists until we were finished.

My list looked like this:	My wife's list looked like this:
Warm climate	Good churches
Low traffic	Family friendly
Good country club	Good schools
Major college in town	Yoga / food / music
Nice restaurants/breweries	Mountains within two hours
Airport within 1.5 hours	

We did our research and found Raleigh, North Carolina; Asheville, North Carolina; and Athens, Georgia.

Right away, we discovered that Asheville's airport was too small, and Raleigh was too expensive. But in Athens, we could buy a four-bedroom, new-build house ten minutes from downtown for less than $300,000. On our second visit, we put in an offer on a home and moved.

It was the best decision we ever made.

My advice:

Have the courage to find a new place to live with more of what you want. Don't feel tied to where you were raised.

Friendships

People brag about the weather in San Diego. The opportunity in New York City. The food scene in Houston. The outdoor adventures in

Colorado. The fishing in Key West. The energy in college towns. The list goes on . . .

But what they don't tell you is that the most important part of any city you choose is the community. Your friends. The people who you spend time with. Great people can make any city great. No friends at all can make any region brutal.

Making friends takes work.

If you aren't willing to do the work, you won't make any friends in a new environment and you will be miserable.

A lot of lonely people on social media complain about not having any friends but make zero effort to do things with people. If you sit in your house playing video games or watching Netflix, you will not make friends. If you wait for people to come up to you and invite you to do things, it won't happen.

When we moved to Athens, Georgia, we didn't know anybody within three hours. Not a single person.

Today, seven years later, we have an amazing community of friends we do everything with, from vacationing to playing golf to getting coffee and dinner. Our kids play together. Our community is strong!

My advice:

Bring energy to conversations and ask people about themselves. Approach people your age and strike up conversations. Ask other grown adults for their phone numbers and invite them to do things like play golf or get dinner. Say yes when people invite you to things even if you don't feel like going.

Read the book *The 7 Habits of Highly Effective People*—a self-help classic.

It works. We made friends this way, and they are a super-important part of our life.

Marriage and Family

I'm of the opinion people are waiting way too long to get married and have children. They keep working and dating and traveling and putting off making the sacrifice because it isn't a priority.

That is a massive mistake.

My advice:

Get married young and have more kids than you can afford.

I have been able to accomplish a lot more in business and in life since I married my wife and had kids with her. Priorities shift in a whole new way, and you refocus on productive habits that are more beneficial to you and everyone around you. There is a level of discipline that is required in marriage and parenting that bleeds over in good ways to other areas of life. Especially your career.

One of the big problems is the illusion of infinite choice. Dating apps where there is always somebody new to meet and have dinner with or date for a little while. Cities full of thirty-five to forty-five-year-old single people.

In my opinion this is a total disaster.

Having kids gets harder when you are older. Changing your ways and settling down gets harder if you've spent twenty years dating different people and doing whatever you want all the time.

We've also been sold on this idea that "getting it out of your system" is a good plan. The travel. The sleeping around. The freedom.

In reality, it doesn't work this way. It builds bad habits and delays one of the most rewarding things about life:

Children.

Something amazing happens when you have kids:

You grow up. You mature. You get better at life. You make better decisions. You make more money. I don't know if it's evolution or a natural occurrence, but it is very real. I got better at all aspects of life when I got married and had kids.

I've never met anyone who wishes they'd had fewer kids. But I've met a lot of people who regret waiting so long and wish they'd had more kids.

Every person I know over fifty years old cares about one thing above all else:

Their kids and grandkids.

There is also an illusion of "perfection" that exists as you keep looking and dating and looking and dating. In reality most people would be much better off finding somebody with two traits and getting married:

1. You can trust them. They are morally sound and share your values.
2. They keep calm under pressure, and they are emotionally stable.

The trust one is obvious. The second one is the one a lot of people mess up.

Life gets hard especially when you have kids, jobs, a house to care for, responsibilities, and so on. If your spouse is an emotional mess every time something stressful happens, you're in for a long road. Date somebody long enough to figure out how they operate under pressure and then get married if you are happy with the result.

And an important reminder:

Just like your employees, your spouse will not change once you get married.

It is unbelievable how many people expect this to happen. If you date somebody who likes to go to boutiques and spend thousands of dollars a month, they'll also be poor managers of money when you get married. Same with partying, watching football all day every Sunday, eating crappy food, not exercising, sports betting, or whatever else.

Do not try to change people. Find a person with good habits and similar priorities right off the bat.

Parenthood

I think a lot of parents today are raising soft kids and it is a disaster.

They do everything in their power to protect their children from pain, mistakes, and suffering. What we're left with is a lot of kids who are sixteen years old and can't do anything but look down at their phones and scroll social media.

Zero personality. Zero communication skills. Zero work ethic. No money or job prospects after college. And the worst part is these kids have no ability to solve their own problems or make their own decisions.

Unfortunately, life will not be kind to these kids.

If you make every decision for your child and bail them out every time they mess up, they will be totally unable to hack it in this world once they go out on their own.

I've met a lot of spoiled brats who had rich parents. No understanding of the value of a dollar. No ability to work hard. Always given everything in life and a complete drain on society. But I've also met a lot of exceptionally humble and productive people who came from serious money. When I meet these folks, I always ask the parents what they did to raise such good kids.

The answers always revolve around the following theme:

Teach your kids to struggle with grace.

Let them practice messing up and don't bail them out. Encourage and support them, but do not shelter them from the real world by doing their college applications for them, micromanaging their homework, trying to protect them from anything evil in the world, and so on and so forth.

I think this is incredibly important.

Here is the deal:

Life is hard for everyone. No matter how rich you are, you will still suffer. You'll still get sick on vacation. You'll end up with some health problems. Every job is hard. Relationships are hard. Fitness is hard. Staying away from all the addictive substances and activities is hard. Discipline is hard.

If you don't give your children any practice dealing with difficulty, they won't learn how to do it.

Too many parents do everything for their kids. They never tell them no when they are toddlers or kids because they don't want them to cry. They sit and help them with homework. They write their college essays. As soon as a kid steps out of line, they reel them right back in before they ever make a mistake.

So the kids never have to deal with stress or pressure or pain. But dealing with stress and pain is a muscle. You have to do it over and over again before it eventually gets easier and maybe one day doesn't really rattle you at all.

My advice:

Let your kids make good and bad decisions when they are young and the stakes are low.

Let them fail and deal with the minor consequences of their poor choices. Let them practice making decisions that increase slowly over time in importance and magnitude. That way, when they get out into the real world, they can hack it, and they are comfortable.

Make them get a job to earn money and learn responsibility. Make them look people in the eye and teach them how to have a conversation and ask questions.

Do not let your kids get into video games. It is a terrible habit and leads to kids having no desire to get outside, have adventures, or play real sports.

There won't be a video game system in my home under any circumstances. Plus if you can keep your kids from getting into video games before the age of about sixteen, they'll be so far behind their friends it won't be fun for them. The chances will be virtually zero that your kids grow up to be adults who spend twenty hours a week on a computer casting spells.

Be consistent.

Young kids need consistency. Don't spank your kids out of anger. Don't lash out at your kids. Don't yell at them. *If you can't control your emotions, how do you expect them to control theirs?* If kids know what to expect and know what battles you are going to consistently fight, they will begin to comply and listen to you as parents.

Teach your children about business and the way entrepreneurship works. Talk to them about how businesses make money. Let them get a taste of selling something and making a profit for themselves at a young age.

The truth is that wealth stays in families and is passed down from generation to generation because of what is taught and learned around the dinner table. Entrepreneurial culture is much more likely to be adopted by kids who have entrepreneurial parents. One of the greatest gifts you can give to your children is a look at how business works and the opportunity to build something of their own.

Finally, build your kids up.

So many parents are so hard on their kids when it comes to achieving at all costs. It's ridiculous, especially when it comes to youth sports. I had friends growing up who simply couldn't perform on the basketball court because their parents yelled at them after every game.

My dad was hard on me in a lot of ways, but he never tore me down. He always made me believe I belonged, had talent and skill, and was good at what I was trying to do. That made a huge difference for me.

You can start this at a very young age.

Every night right before they fall asleep, I ask my kids if they want me to tell them a story or tell them all the things I love about them.

They pick the love, and I go on to compliment them for about thirty seconds straight. *I love how hard you tried today when we were swinging the golf club. I love how nice you are to your sister. I love how you always listen to Mommy when she asks you to do something. I love how fast you can run.*

I build them up and give them confidence, and it bleeds over to every part of their lives. They absolutely love it.

To this day, they've never asked me for a story.

Adventure

Adventure is a requirement.

Packing a tent on my back and walking into the wilderness with close friends is amazing. Suffering up a mountain on a bicycle is a religious experience for me. Finding a hole in a creek way out in the middle of nowhere and pulling out a trout is a rush. Sitting in a tree stand while a big whitetail buck walks underneath and then harvesting it with my bow makes me feel alive.

Men need adventure.

We need to push ourselves. We need to get out in nature and get uncomfortable to reset our dopamine receptors and keep a calm perspective when things get stressful at work or at home.

Embrace this.

Go chase the elk. Go up the mountain. Dive in the ocean with a spear gun chasing the fish.

Share the experience with your kids and your friends. It will make you a better person and a stronger human.

Conclusion

Nobody gave me permission to get rich.

I didn't have a background in real estate. I didn't come from a real estate family. My father worked for a developer for a salary and never owned a rental property. My mother was a school nurse. I didn't get a job offer to work at a real estate PE firm out of college. If I had asked to work for Sam Zell as a twenty-year-old, he would have said no.

I didn't have permission to jump into the real estate business. I didn't have the right résumé. I didn't have the experience. I didn't have the knowledge. I didn't have that stamp of approval from a top real estate college or pass an exam to become a licensed real estate agent.

But here I am.

The owner of a real estate private equity firm with no boss. I acquired and control more than $150 million worth of real estate. I also own stakes in several companies that are growing fast.

Nobody gave me permission to do any of this risky, hard, uncomfortable stuff.

Nobody is going to give you permission to do what you want to do either.

If you're looking to do it the traditional way—study the thing, get an internship in the thing, wait for somebody to tell you you're qualified to do the thing, and get a good job doing that thing—entrepreneurship is not for you.

You see this insecurity all over the business world.

I'm not qualified. I'm not prepared. How can I take this on when I don't have any experience?

There is no textbook with all the answers. You have to figure them out as you go along. You have to stop worrying about qualifications and ignore the people telling you what you can or can't do. Most problems aren't straightforward. Life isn't always logical. You can't pull up YouTube and watch a how-to guide or look at the little book that came with the pack of Legos.

Successful folks don't need all the answers. They don't need instructions either. They attack problems, and they figure things out. They go after opportunities they aren't qualified for. They give themselves permission.

If you're sitting back waiting for somebody to tell you you're allowed to launch your business and you're qualified enough to make it work, it isn't going to happen.

You have to give yourself permission.

It takes a while to stop feeling like an impostor. I still feel like one to this day.

I don't belong here. What makes me qualified to build businesses and buy real estate? I'm just a guy.

Impostor syndrome hits everyone. No matter how cool, calm, and collected they might look under pressure, they feel it.

LeBron feels it. Musk feels it. The president feels it.

It pops up at the most inconvenient times, usually right before a very big, high-pressure moment. It's a voice in my head telling me to run back to safety. Asking me why I decided to put myself in the spotlight.

Why in the world did I choose to do this uncomfortable, scary stuff? You can't do this. You aren't smart enough. You aren't athletic enough. You aren't a good enough leader. You aren't brilliant enough.

We all feel this. We all have that lizard brain in the back of our minds telling us to run from the danger. It isn't logical. Nobody cares if you succeed or fail. Nobody is watching you or worrying about you or calling you names when you underperform.

Everybody is worried about themselves. They are thinking about what they're having for dinner. Or worried about making rent. Or stressed out over any number of other things.

I know a ton of incompetent people who make phenomenal money simply because they aren't insecure. I also know a ton of very competent people who fail over and over again to reach their true potential because they are.

So how do you get over this impostor syndrome?

First, you acquire the network, skills, and capital. But, of course, it's more than that.

It's practice.

Believing in yourself is never easy. So put yourself in as many difficult situations as you can. Train your lizard brain to get back in its cage and leave you alone. Learn to love the pressure and the rush you get when there is potential for humiliation or failure.

People generally care a lot less about you than you think they do. The people who care about you do so because they have something to gain by you being around. They don't care if you are qualified. They have a problem they need solved. They don't care if you know what you're doing. If you act like it and can give it a valiant effort, they'll probably give you a shot.

Repeat after me:

I will not reinvent the wheel.
I will copy what works.
I will use proven methods to make money in boring ways.
I will do common things uncommonly well.
If it isn't broken, I will not try to fix it.
I will keep it simple.

Repeat it. Repeat it again. Then get out there and get rich doing boring things.

Acknowledgments

My entrepreneurial journey has been full of highs and lows. I would like to express my deepest gratitude for those people who have stood beside me through the roller-coaster ride.

To my wife, Michelle, for her love and support.

To my children for their energy and unconditional love.

To my parents, Tim and Susan, for raising me around a dinner table of positivity and curiosity. They made me feel as if I could accomplish anything and taught me to see the world through a lens of opportunity.

To my business partner, Dan Hagberg, who has been through hell with me and made it out the other side.

To Colin Campbell and Julie Mosow for turning a bunch of ideas into this book.

About the Author

Nick Huber is an entrepreneur who resides in Athens, Georgia, with his wife and three children. He owns Somewhere.com, Bolt Storage, RE Cost Seg, and several other businesses. At the time of this writing, his real-estate portfolio includes sixty-eight self-storage properties and more than two million square feet. His portfolio of companies employs over 325 people and does over $30 million in annual revenue. Nick enjoys golf, hunting, mountain biking, history, fishing, travel, sports and spending time outside with his friends and family.